11/02

5.12   10   2/11

Palo Alto City Library

The individual borrower is responsible for all library material borrowed on his or her card.

Charges as determined by the CITY OF PALO ALTO will be assessed for each overdue item.

Damaged or non-returned property will be billed to the individual borrower by the CITY OF PALO ALTO.

P.O. Box 10250, Palo Alto, CA 94303

A DOUBLE THREAD

A Double Thread

Growing Up English and Jewish in London

JOHN GROSS

Ivan R. Dee
CHICAGO

First published in Great Britain by Chatto & Windus.

ISBN 1-56663-424-5

The Library of Congress CIP data is available under LC 2001047577.

To Tom and Susanna

Contents

A Note on the American Edition

At one stage I thought of calling this book *An English Childhood*. There would have been deliberate irony in the choice of such a title, given all the elements in my background and upbringing that were not English, or far from typically so; but beyond that there would also have been a recognition of the extent to which the childhood that the book describes was distinctively and irrevocably English nonetheless.

It seems a fair assumption that the Englishness of an English story will be more apparent to American readers than to local ones. Many things that English readers take for granted – the ballast of the book, so to speak – are likely to strike Americans as exotic; even experiences that Americans share are likely to sound curiously different when they are recounted in an English accent. And while it is perhaps not for the author to say, a good deal of whatever interest the book has for Americans must surely lie in this "foreign" aspect.

The story does have its American elements, however, and if I had been initially writing for an American audience I would have been tempted to make more of them. I have said something in the pages that follow of the impact of American popular culture during my childhood – of films, above all, but also of songs, comic strips, magazines, stories. I could have said much more. And beyond the products of the entertainment industry there were jokes, fashions, slang, packaging, a whole mass of American lore. I never had a single lesson in American history while I was at school, and I have never met an English contemporary who did.

But America was by a long stretch the foreign country we were most aware of – often, of course, in fantasy form.

The spread of American influence had been a familiar story long before World War II, but for an English child growing up during and just after the war it was peculiarly intense. America was our ally. At a time of shortages and restrictions, it stood out more than ever as the land of plenty. It was also synonymous with power – with Joe Louis, big cars, the Empire State Building, and in due course, for better or worse, with the atomic bomb.

Not everyone approved. Objections floated down from the adult world – political criticisms from the left, disdain for American vulgarity from the right. But among children, if I am in any way representative, the image was overwhelmingly favorable. America stood for streamlining and the open road, for excitement and optimism. "Color by Technicolor" – the colors seemed twice as bright when they were spelled in the American fashion. And how right it seemed that the most famous hangout of GIs in London during the war should have been called Rainbow Corner.

True, even children had an alternative image, in large part fostered by comic strips and comedians. We knew that Americans were also somehow absurd – that they had names like Elmer and Hiram, and talked about "ornery critters," and said things like "Aw, shucks, honey"; that they were forever chewing gum and handing out sticks of it in an effort to win friends. (If there had been an anti-globalization campaign in those days, it would have gone after Wrigley's rather than Starbucks or McDonald's.) But the caricatures were often tinged with affection, and sometimes there was even an odd blending of traditions. One of the two or three most memorable icons thrown up by the English comics I read as a child – I talk about him in the book – was stubble-chinned Desperate Dan. He was unmistakably a cowboy, yet he was somehow English too; at any rate, he had a lot more in common with a figure out of an English pantomime or music-hall turn than he did with Hopalong Cassidy or Gene Autry.

We were also exposed to more elevated aspects of American culture. It wasn't altogether an accident that when I began reading poetry, one of my treasured volumes was a secondhand Longfellow. (In terms of sales he was the most popular living poet in Victorian England — more popular even than Tennyson.) It seemed entirely natural that one of the first poems the most staunchly English and patriotic of my teachers read aloud to the class should have been Whittier's "Barbara Frietchie." And then there were the American children's classics. The chief impression they left me with was that of an idyll. I knew that bad things happened in *Tom Sawyer*, and sad things in *Little Women*, but a small American town still seemed a singularly attractive place to be.

The anti-idylls came later — *Babbitt* and *Winesburg, Ohio* and my own somber favorite Theodore Dreiser. And then there were . . . But I hope I have said enough to suggest how far images of America could help to shape an English upbringing, even fifty or sixty years ago.

I should add that in my own case the process was reinforced by my Jewish background. Many English Jews had American family connections. (It was an exciting day when one of my mother's cousins from Rye, New York, showed up in clean-cut U.S. army uniform — this was not long before the end of the war — and discoursed about the glories of American ice cream.) Many English Jews must likewise have speculated about what would have happened if their parents or grandparents had followed the usual course and landed in New York rather than London. Bits of American-Jewish folklore drifted across the ocean: Manischewitz, Grossinger, Molly Picon were names that meant something. After the war, when big American variety stars came over to the Palladium, Jews were famously well represented in the audience. (At one time the cult of Danny Kaye assumed something like religious proportions.) And in business, "American" implied the last word in modernity. Many a shoe shop or men's outfitters in the East End and North London gave itself a lift by claiming that its fashions came direct from Florida or California.

Among the letters I received after the British edition of *A Double Thread* appeared, one made me realize I had probably been propagating an Anglo-American urban myth, and another put me right on a basic piece of family history.

In Chapter Six, recalling "Uncle Mac" of the BBC program *Children's Hour*, I cite the story of the occasion when someone supposedly failed to turn off the microphone, and Uncle Mac was overheard referring to the juvenile listeners whom he had just wished a sonorous goodnight as "little buggers." A friend, Nelson Polsby of the University of California, wrote to me pointing out that essentially the same story had once been widely current in the States. He also supplied chapter and verse, from Gerald Nachman's *Raised on Radio* (1998) – a passage in which Nachman records the popular belief that Don Carney, who was host of the New York children's show *Uncle Don* in the 1930s and '40s, once "cracked into an open mike, 'That oughta hold the little bastards for a while!'"

The second letter I have mentioned was from a distant cousin on my mother's side, a lady somewhat older than me, whom I had never really known. In addition to supplying some vivid fragments of family history, she told me that before migrating to London my mother's family had lived in a town in the province of Vitebsk, in Belarus, and not – as my mother had told me, and as I say in the book – in Lithuania.

I should add that I can't recall my mother ever having spoken about the subject when I was young. When I finally asked her about it she was in her eighties, and fairly vague: "Lithuania" was not so much an answer as a suggestion. But then I can't recall any of my other relatives speaking about it, either. Some Jewish families retained lively memories of the towns or districts they had come from in Eastern Europe, most obviously when they formed communal associations or *landsmanshaftn*. Others were quite willing to forget.

Would it have made a difference if I had grown up with some memory of Vitebsk, however slight, hovering in the background? Possibly. The very name Vitebsk has a touch of magic about it, thanks to its associations with Marc Chagall. But it was not to be. And as for the mistake about Lithuania – it is regrettable; but it is not a point I dwell on, and I don't think it seriously distorts anything else in the story.

J. G.

A DOUBLE THREAD

Preface

This book is the story of my early life, up to the age of seventeen. That means that it is also the story of the two separate but entwined legacies of being English and being Jewish. Hence my title: *A Double Thread*.

The changes of the past generation have done a good deal to erode the English sense of identity. Fifty or sixty years ago there was a much firmer idea of what being English meant, even among those who rejected it or sought to change it. And this was the world in which I grew up, and whose customs and assumptions I absorbed with the air I breathed. 'England made me.'

At the same time it was impressed upon me from the earliest days that being Jewish was one of the central facts of my existence. Perhaps the same is true of the great majority of Jews – or was, during the Hitler era. But there are degrees of Jewishness, and two circumstances combined to strengthen my commitment. In the first place, my family was Orthodox in principle, and semi-Orthodox in practice: religion underlay our lives. Second, my father's family were relative latecomers to England. My father had been born and spent his childhood in Eastern Europe, in a world which was very remote from my own, yet with which I felt (on occasion) a strong emotional bond.

In describing this mixed inheritance and how it worked itself out, I have concentrated as much on atmosphere as on incident, on social setting as on anecdote. The book is an account of a childhood in which beliefs and a sense of cultural differences played a large part. To some extent, which may give it a representative value, it is meant be a record of those beliefs and of the attitudes or feelings which went with them.

But no life is ever merely representative. Broad social patterns give this book its framework, but it is also, I hope, a demonstration of how those patterns were constantly modified by accident and circumstance, by personal interests and individual temperament. To devote a whole book to one's childhood – unless it was a childhood marked by great external dramas, which I can't claim – is inevitably to lay oneself open to charges of being self-absorbed. But no memoir is worth writing unless it has the courage of its uniqueness, and if it isn't self-absorbed it is nothing at all.

A number of friends have given me valuable assistance or editorial advice. I would particularly like to thank Jenny Uglow, Miriam Gross and Neil Kozodoy.

I am grateful to the following for permission to reproduce copyright material: Carcanet Press for quotation from *The Terrible Shears* by D.J. Enright; Faber and Faber for quotations from 'The Price' by W.H. Auden, 'Burnt Norton' and 'Burbank with a Baedeker' by T.S. Eliot, and David Higham Associates for 'Sunday Morning' by Louis MacNeice. Part of Chapter 15 first appeared, in a somewhat different form, in *Commentary* (New York), and is reprinted by kind permission of the editor and publishers.

I

Immigrants

'You're such a *lobbes*!' It is a cousin speaking to me. She is eight or nine, I am three or four, so the year is probably 1939. I realise from her tone that the remark is an affectionate rebuke – so affectionate that it is scarcely a rebuke at all. *Lobbes* means something like 'rascal'. Do I also realise that it isn't an English word, but a Yiddish one? I'm not sure. What I *do* know is that, even though I understand it, it strikes me as a very strange word. I am fascinated by its shape and sound; it reminds me of 'lobster'. And that begins to raise disturbing possibilities. Do I really want to be compared to a creature as weird as a lobster? (Perhaps, for good measure, I already know that according to Jewish law lobsters are forbidden food.) Everything else is lost in a haze, but my sense of puzzlement must have gone deep: the tiny incident still stands out sharp and clear.

My father was born in Gorokhov, a small town in Volhynia – a region straddling south-east Poland and the western Ukraine – in 1899 or 1900. The family took in lodgers and traded in feeding-stuff for animals. Whether they had any other means of support, I was never told, and never felt impelled to ask – not, at any rate, until long after my father was dead and it was too late. In 1913 they emigrated to England. Again, I know nothing of the circumstances, other than that they slipped across the frontier of what was still the Russian Empire by night; that my father, the oldest of four children, carried a small brother on his back as they did; and that they boarded ship at Bremen (a town chiefly memorable to my father as the first place where he tasted ic

3

cream). Arriving in London, my grandparents settled in the East End, and somehow scraped together enough money to start a small, never very flourishing grocery. (Someone once described it to me as the kind of shop which people would pop into for a cupful of rice.) It was in Cannon Street Road, in the shadow of St George's in the East, one of the three great churches which Nicholas Hawksmoor built in east London in the early eighteenth century.

Why England? In the tide of Jewish emigration from Eastern Europe which began in the 1880s, as a result of intensified anti-Semitism and anti-Jewish decrees, the dreamed-of destination was overwhelmingly America. Some Jews who fetched up in England had originally thought of it as a halfway house. Others had been cheated by unscrupulous travel agents: the tickets which were supposed to take them to New York only got them as far as London. But there were no stories of this kind in my family, and no talk of America as an opportunity missed. Nor were there any close family members already established in England, who might have served as an advance guard. *Something* must have persuaded my grandparents to take this path rather than that path, possibly a quite small consideration; what it was remains a mystery.

Another question mark hangs over the family name. In one or two official documents, dating from their early years in England, it appears in alternative versions, as 'Grosser or Gross'. In practice, it is true, they opted firmly for 'Gross', so the mystery is only a very minor one. Yet every now and then, when I was young, the possibility that I might have been called Grosser set me musing.

For a start, it would have meant that I wouldn't have been exposed to the playground jokes about being 'gross'. (I would no doubt have had to put up with jokes about grocers instead, but they would almost certainly have been preferable.) And I was intrigued for another, less obvious reason. As 'John Grosser' I would have been virtually the namesake of a legendary East End figure, Father John Groser, an Anglo-Catholic priest (his duties included taking charge of St George's in the East after it had been bombed in the Blitz) and dedicated Christian socialist. Not that I would necessarily have welcomed this. On the contrary, the feeling that the possibility produced, as is often the case with namesakes,

4

was rather disconcerting – all the more so since Groser was widely regarded, even by those who disagreed with him politically, as a near saint. His long craggy features are preserved for posterity in the 1951 film of *Murder in the Cathedral*, in which he played Becket. Anyone looking less like a *lobbes* it would be hard to imagine.

Possibly the confusion over names derived from nothing more than an immigration officer's mistake, a foreign name misheard and scribbled down in a hurry; either way it came to symbolise in my mind the disruptive effects of immigration, its disarray. And it made my father's other name, his Hebrew name, seem rock-solid by contrast. Avraham ben Oser – Abraham the son of Oser (a variant on Ezra, meaning 'help'): here at least were certainty and continuity.

My father's parents were deeply religious. Their lives were bounded by Jewish law and ritual; their days were largely built around a Jewish timetable. For my grandfather, that meant not only the festivals, major and minor, but three sets of daily prayers – *shachris* in the morning, *mincha* in the afternoon, *ma'ariv* in the evening. The Sabbath, of course, was central. My grandmother kept a scrupulously kosher home; and outside that home much the most important focus of their existence was *shul*, the synagogue.

None of this was extraordinary: countless Jewish immigrants from Eastern Europe arrived in the West sharing the same degree of belief. What was more unusual, perhaps, was the tenacity with which they went on clinging to the old ways. Their youngest son, the most obviously go-ahead of their children, once remarked to me, with a touch of affection but rather more exasperation, 'They just tried to go on as though they were still in Gorokhov.' But then they had settled in England at an age at which it was unlikely that they were going to change very much. I know that my grandmother was in her late thirties; my grandfather must have been in his early forties.

They took it for granted that they could transmit their beliefs to their children. To a considerable extent they succeeded. And in the case of my father, their hopes went further – not only because he was the oldest, but also because from an early age he had shown signs of being a gifted student. Without any claim to being scholars themselves, they revered scholarship – by which they essentially meant the study of the Talmud and its commentators – as a supreme Jewish pursuit. My father had begun studying in a yeshiva, a Talmudic college, before the family left Poland, and when they arrived in London one of the first things his mother did – she seems to have been the one who took the big decisions – was to haul him round to the nearest equivalent she could find, the Yeshiva Ets Chaim in Whitechapel. He was a modest man, but in later life he couldn't conceal a certain pride in recalling the interview which followed. The head of the yeshiva had initially been sceptical about whether he would be up to the standard required. It had taken only a couple of minutes' questioning for him to change his mind.

'Ets Chaim' means 'the tree of life': the Law, as it says in the Book of Proverbs, 'is a tree of life to them that grasp it'. Some fifty years after my father studied there, I sought out the site of the yeshiva. The building was derelict (though you could still make out its name in Hebrew characters over the door), but it can never have been a very imposing structure in its prime – a dingy building in a small dingy street. Yet wits were sharpened there, passions were kindled, ancient traditions were preserved.

The Talmud was to remain a closed book to me – or rather, a whole series of closed books; but that doesn't mean that I didn't acquire a looming sense of its significance, and of the role it played among the devout. My father's references to it, however casual, implied an entire way of life. To analyse the sacred texts, to enlarge, to extrapolate, to interpret and reinterpret, to make connections and establish distinctions – the student rejoiced in the task, and rejoiced that it was endless. A phrase I heard quoted more than once was 'the sea of the Talmud'. The sea stretched to the horizon; it got deeper the further out you went.

At the same time I could hardly fail to be aware that among its critics the Talmud was associated with arid legalism and hair-splitting. The short answer to such accusations (since the critics seemed to have no trouble in producing examples of what they meant) was that it contained lots of other things as well. I at least learned enough at second-hand to know that it was a whole literature rather than a single book; that along with its legal elements (the Halachah), it consisted of a mass of ethical reflections, folklore, prayers, parables, records, legends and imaginative speculations (the Haggadah). It would have been out of character for my father not to have appreciated this more imaginative and emotion-charged material; equally, I don't think he would have denied that the dialectical swordplay of the Talmud sometimes degenerated into mere ingenuity. But overall, as far as I can judge, the Halachah still gave him at least as much pleasure as the Haggadah. When he spoke of a Talmudic passage 'tasting good' (having a *gute ta'am*), he could have been thinking of either.

Although study at a yeshiva was engaged in for its own sake, as its own reward, it could obviously lead on to a career as a rabbi, and the next step my father took – enrolling as a student at Jews' College, which at that time was in Queen Square, Bloomsbury – looked like a move in the same direction. Founded in 1855 (at a later date it would no doubt have been given a less brusque name), the college was a seminary designed to turn out ministers on the approved Anglo-Jewish model. But for some of its students from immigrant homes it also served as a bridge to a wider English world, and the professions, and so it proved with my father. In his case, that meant medicine. He was accepted by St Bartholomew's Hospital, 'Bart's', in Smithfield – an unusual achievement at the time for a student with his kind of background – and embarked on the long slog of medical training, partly supporting himself by giving Hebrew lessons, almost always walking from Whitechapel to the hospital and back in order to save the fare. In 1925, not long after qualifying, he set up in practice in Mile End, where he was to work and make his home for the rest of his life. Unlike most of his Jewish contemporaries – unlike his own parents – he never left the East End.

Life as a doctor brought him into much greater contact with non-Jews, especially among his patients. It also made inroads into his Jewish commitments. Strict observance of the Sabbath was no longer feasible, for instance. (There were surgeries on Saturday mornings and Saturday nights in those days – and on Sunday mornings, for that matter.) Quite possibly, too, his whole outlook was subtly modified. Yet his essential loyalties remained firm. He prayed; he observed the major Jewish laws as best he could; he even occasionally found time to 'run off' (as he would have put it) to a *shiur*, an informal Talmudic study group.

He had been in medical practice for almost a decade before he got married. My mother, Muriel, who was twelve years younger, had been born in England: on her mother's side she came from a large family, originally from Lithuania, which had settled in London shortly before the turn of the century. The men – her mother was one of eleven brothers and sisters – were mostly furriers; they were hard-headed types who knew how to make a decent living, and at a fairly early stage they had got away from the East End, trekking north (a common route for their generation) towards the more spacious regions of Dalston, Stoke Newington and Stamford Hill.

In terms of his early background, then, and of foreignness, my father was less a contemporary of my mother than of her parents and uncles and aunts. Even that doesn't tell the whole story. My mother's grandparents had been devout Jews, on the standard East European model. Their children kept up some of the old ways, and were of course unmistakably Jewish, but (as far as I could judge) they weren't attached to their Jewishness with any great warmth. Certainly religion played far less part in their lives than it did in my father's. It is a mark of how far they had moved on that the eldest of the brothers, the head of the clan, left instructions that he should be cremated – something which on religious grounds would have been unthinkable in my father's family.

Whatever their differences from him, the assembled uncles and aunts liked my father and made him welcome. They were great card players, and a regular feature of my childhood was hanging around on family visits while the grown-ups got on with their poker or solo or whatever. Sometimes a relative would take pity on me and invite me to join him, or more likely her, in a simple card game: there was a particularly elementary one, just about my level, called pishi-paisha. But I never much liked cards, then or later, and preferred to read the papers or eavesdrop on the adults. Between games and during pauses there was a lot of family gossip, the more interesting to me for being only half-understood, and sporadic talk about politics. I can recall Hitler's name being mentioned with a curse.

These were lively enough gatherings (for the adults, at least); yet I couldn't help sensing a deeper rapport on the relatively infrequent occasions when my father played cards with one of my mother's cousins (actually, one of *her* mother's cousins), a timber merchant called Moshay who lived in a large gloomy house in Willesden. Moshay was a student of the Talmud too – he had a set of Talmudic tractates in his living room, formidable volumes which were propped on the floor under a bookcase because they were too tall to fit on the shelves; and though he was a genial and worldly man, you were never left in any doubt that he took his religion seriously. Once, while we were visiting him, he remonstrated with one of the other players in a game of cards for exclaiming '*Gottenyu!*' – literally, 'Our God' – after a run of bad luck. It wasn't exactly a full-blown sin, you were made to feel, but it was a bit like saying 'Oh, Christ!' in the presence of the Archbishop of Canterbury.

I found Moshay an impressive figure; I warmed to him on my father's account. But from my own point of view the qualities which drew my father to him also constituted a barrier. The two of them often slipped into speaking Yiddish, which I couldn't understand; I knew even then that I was never going to venture on to 'the sea of the Talmud'; there was the strong sense of a shared past which left me feeling excluded. My one improbable consolation was an oil painting which hung in the hall, and which I kept returning to – an Alpine lake, with the moon shining down from a starry sky. It was probably even more chocolate-boxy than I recall, but at the time it seemed extraordinarily romantic.

I have not so far mentioned my mother's father – which is a reflection of how things were (or at any rate how they struck me when I was a child). He died long before I was born, and of all the figures in the story he remains the most shadowy. Jacob Felkoff: the very name, as I write it down, seems almost that of a stranger. And yet it is a name which binds me to him. Following the Jewish custom of naming a child after a relative who is no longer living, I was given Jacob as my own second name – in Hebrew, and in English too, which made a difference. Fashions in names have changed, and in recent years 'Jacob' has come back into use among the population at large; but when I was young and had to give my full name (on a form, for instance), it was an unmistakable proclamation of Jewishness.

Like his in-laws, Jacob Felkoff was a furrier. He came from Russia, had a workshop off Petticoat Lane, and lived for some years in Goodman's Fields (a tiny area just east of the City, famous in the annals of the theatre as the site of the playhouse where David Garrick first appeared on stage). After his death he left behind the reputation of having a been a good husband and father, but beyond that – in my presence, at least – he was hardly ever spoken of. One of the few things I know about him is that he was a staunch supporter of the Labour Party: he read the *Daily Herald* and subscribed to *Lansbury's Labour Weekly* (though he must sometimes have taken the *Daily Mirror* as well, since as a girl my mother was devoted to the *Mirror* comic strip 'Pip, Squeak and Wilfred'). I have only two mementoes of him – apart from my name, that is. One is a broken-backed *machzor*, or prayer book for the festivals, with his name firmly inscribed with a thick-nibbed pen. The other is a pencilled note addressed to my mother, written in hospital while he lay dying, full of fatherly concern.

My grandmother, widowed in her forties, was a short, sturdy, fresh-complexioned woman who played a considerable part in my childhood, and on the whole a bright one. She had the knack of telling stories, entering into games and generally keeping you entertained; one of her specialities was baking *taigelach* – small treacle-coated biscuits which no dentist could have approved of and few children would have been able to resist. Occasionally, she talked about Russia. I was particularly impressed to learn, at an early age, that the peasants used to call the Tsar 'Little Father'. Later, my sense of something Russian trailing away in the background was reinforced by the presence in her house of one or two Russian books (in translation). In particular there was a novel, which I often sneaked a look at, Alexander Kuprin's *Yama: The Pit.* (What chiefly attracted me were its descriptions of a brothel.) Still, Russianness, real or supposed, was only a small element in the picture. There were other, more frequent times when she seemed to me thoroughly English – when she sang snatches of Boer War songs, for instance, which she must have picked up during her early years here. The one I enjoyed most

contained a promise to 'make old Kruger suck a lollipop' when the
war was over.

My mother's upbringing took the process of anglicisation much
further. She won a scholarship to a grammar school; today, she
would almost certainly have gone on to a university, and even at
the time, if she had been a boy, she might have stood a chance. But
for a girl of her generation, unless she was a positive high-flyer, the
prospect didn't arise, and she ended up as a shorthand typist
instead.

The one field in which she showed unusual promise was music.
Her first piano teacher soon passed her on to a second, who was
better qualified. The second one took what was meant to be a
short trip back to Poland, and was never heard of again. But
before he left he had suggested that her parents get in touch with
Tobias Matthay, one of the most celebrated music teachers of the
day, and in due course she was awarded a place at the Matthay
school in Wimpole Street.

Matthay went back a long way. He himself had been a pupil of
Sterndale Bennett and Arthur Sullivan, and by the time my mother
got to know him he had become a figure of legend, 'Uncle Tobs'.
She had a splendid photograph of him, seated at the piano,
looking every inch the velvet-jacketed maestro; she was proud of
having played in a concert given by his pupils at the Wigmore Hall
when she was only nine or ten. Eventually, alas, she abandoned
her studies. But for many years playing still meant a good deal to
her, and the Bechstein which my father bought for her not long
after they were married was a much-prized possession – not just an
instrument, but a symbol, in the way that pianos used to be, of
civilised aspirations. Luckily, my parents were unaware that the
Bechstein family had been among Hitler's most important early
patrons.

It took me a long time to recognise that our home was much
more traditional than it would have been if my mother had been
left to her own devices. My parents were a devoted couple, who
agreed, or appeared to agree, about most things; if, as a small
child, I had any sense of disparities between them – cultural
disparities, that is – it was largely at second-hand, through my
grandmothers. And *there* the differences were unmistakable,

summed up by the fact that my mother's mother was always known to her grandchildren as 'Grandma', while my father's mother was the traditional East European 'Booba'. It couldn't conceivably have been the other way round.

There was a contrast between their actual names, too. In my mother's family, the women of my grandmother's generation no longer had specifically Jewish names: my grandmother was called Alice. My father's mother, on the other hand, was Pessya – a ghetto or shtetl (small-town) name, fit to stand alongside the Feigas and Gitls and Beilas in the Yiddish tales of Sholem Aleichem.

I mustn't make the differences between the two women sound more extreme than they were. My maternal grandmother still had numerous links with organised Jewish life. (One nephew, bucking the family trend, became a well-known rabbi.) Her talk abounded in Jewish references; and if it wasn't particularly peppered with Yiddishisms, there were times when only Yiddish would do. When she was in hospital in her eighties, enduring her last painful illness, a nurse filling out a form asked her – bureaucratically, preposterously – what had been the cause of her own mother's death. Reverting to the only language that could relieve her feelings, she snapped back that it was because her mother's soul had left her body: '*Di neshome iz aroisgegangen fun dem guf.*'

Yet she always seemed to me to belong essentially to the open world, the world at large. In one of my earliest memories of her she is standing next to Mr Verma, an Indian student who was her lodger at the time. He is laughing (perhaps because I have just told him, as I am told I did, that he looks like a film star); the two of them are plainly on excellent terms.

My father's mother Pessya was at once more formidable and more remote. I have only the dimmest recollection of her husband, 'Zeide' (grandfather), a tallish man with a small beard; by the time I was three or four she too was a widow, installed in a house in Clapton (north of Hackney) with her daughter and her daughter's family. When we visited her I was able to get away and play with my cousins. But as long as she lived she remained the strongest presence in the house, which made the visits something of an ordeal. I shrank inwardly from having to kiss her: her skin felt rough to the touch. Communications were limited, since she had learned (or chose to use) very little English. Above all, there was an intimidating quality about her. I couldn't have put the effect into words at the time, but it was one of admonition. It was as though she were saying – through her looks, through her whole manner – that life, finally, was hard and implacable; that you mustn't put too much trust in your parents' soft reassurances.

Her room was on the first floor, and I have a fixed image of her sitting there on a leather armchair in the semi-gloom. Most of the time the room must have been perfectly well lit, but in memory it always seems sombre, to match her clothes. There are a few gleams – from the fender, perhaps, or from a lampstand – but mostly there are deepening shades of brown, and beyond that dark recesses. The one clear splash of colour I connect with the scene is a picture which hung on the little landing outside, a group of cameos of famous rabbis. The cameos themselves were in sepia or black and white, but each of them had a bright polychrome border. The men they portrayed – one or two of them wearing *shtreimls*, fur hats – were mostly, I imagine, nineteenth-century figures, although the only ones I can remember distinctly are Saadya Gaon (who taught in Babylonia in the tenth century) and the Vilna Gaon (whose life spanned the greater part of the eighteenth century). The Vilna Gaon was an arch-opponent of the revivalist Hassidic movement, incidentally, and of its bias towards intense emotion and mysticism; but although my grandparents' native Volhynia had been one of the regions where the movement had its roots, I was familiar with his name long before I knew that of the founder of Hassidism, the Baal Shem Tov. He was spoken of as the *ne plus ultra* of Jewish learning; he was the scholar who had contrived to keep himself awake so that he could study all night.

My grandmother's slightly flinty manner couldn't disguise the pride she took in any sign of promise I gave. And I never doubted her affection: what made me feel uneasy was that I couldn't love her back as much as I should.

She died at a good age. I was away at boarding school at the time and I was relieved not to be summoned home to the funeral. I knew that my father would be upset, and I didn't think there was anything I could contribute. By chance, however, and without intending to, I supplied a shred of consolation. One of my dreams in those days was of being a political cartoonist, and I used to accompany my weekly letter home with a cartoon inspired by one of the week's events. It was usually meant to be satirical – my model was David Low – but in the week in question Gandhi had been assassinated, and my drawing was an attempt to emulate Low in his solemn vein: it showed a Gandhi-like figure lying in the dust, with gunsmoke drifting above him and a gloomy caption underneath about the fate of the just man. At the time I sent it off, I hadn't heard the news about my grandmother. It reached home the day after she died, and long afterwards my father told me that he had been very touched by it – more, in an odd way, than if I had written a letter about her.

This was five or six weeks before my bar mitzvah. She had already bought me a present, which was duly handed over to me when the time came – a set of *tefillin*, the small boxes containing sacred texts which adult Jewish males are supposed to bind on their foreheads and their left arms during morning prayers. *Tefillin* are known in English as phylacteries, and no translation of a Jewish religious term seems to me to indicate so sharply the gulf between belonging to a tradition and viewing it from outside. 'Phylacteries' sounds technical and outlandish; *tefillin*, to those accustomed to them, sound as natural as your coat or your hat. That didn't mean that, for a young boy, they constituted a particularly exciting present – or, in an era when lavish bar mitzvah presents were already a standing joke, a particularly spectacular one. But for my grandmother they were undoubtedly the most precious gift she could give.

For a week or two during the school holidays which followed, I recited morning prayers (I suppose as a mark of respect to her memory), taking care to put on the *tefillin* the way I had been instructed – winding the end of the strap which went round my arm over the back of my hand, for instance, so that it formed the three-pronged Hebrew letter *shin*. Then I set them aside. At some point, years later – I can't say when – they were either left behind during a move or lost.

2

The Faith of the Fathers

Some years ago there was a British musical about Al Jolson which gave, for a work of its kind, a surprisingly unvarnished account of the singer's meanness and egomania. At one point it showed him talking to his agent, Louis Epstein – the long-suffering 'Eppie' – and launching into a monologue about his family's early days in America: Ellis Island, learning English, the cold-water flat, his parents' piety, every cliché in the immigrant book. Finally, when Eppie could get a word in, he observed with a little sigh, 'Yes, I know, Al, it's a familiar story.' Half-incredulous, the singer fired back: 'You mean I told you already?'

Looking back, a great deal of what once seemed unusual or highly charged about my upbringing, especially my Jewish upbringing, now seems perfectly ordinary. But of course for a child, encountering life for the first time, everything is unique, or retains a sense of its recent uniqueness – all the more so because experience presents itself at that age in such strongly physical terms.

When I think of Sabbath and the festivals, for instance, it is the small incidental impressions which tend to come to mind first. Sabbath means sitting at the dinner table on Friday night, watching melted wax trickle down the side of a candlestick and harden into a blob (so satisfying to peel away afterwards) near the base. Or take the Seder, the meal-cum-service which marks the beginning of Passover. Nothing about it stands out more clearly than the almost inevitable spillage of red wine on a fresh white tablecloth (every glass had to be filled to the brim), and the darker red stains left by fragments of *chrein*, horseradish sauce laced with beetroot.

Another kind of childish fascination attached to the letters of the Hebrew alphabet. I must have learned them not long after I learned the English alphabet, and what chiefly impressed me about them was their shape – the thick and thin strokes, the slight quiffs and curves; that, and the idiosyncratic un-English way in which some of them could behave. I was particularly intrigued by the fact that several of them took on a new elongated form when they came at the end of a word, almost as though they had uncoiled.

If I took a long time to graduate from letters to words and meanings, it is largely because everything was disrupted by the coming of war. We moved home several times between September 1939 and the summer of 1940, and it wasn't until we had settled in Egham, a few miles west of London, that my Jewish education (such as it was) was resumed. There wasn't a Jewish community in the town but for a time there were makeshift Hebrew classes in a borrowed schoolroom, under the auspices of what styled itself – using the traditional term for a Jewish elementary school – a *cheder*. The atmosphere was drab, the textbook we used was depressing: I recall gazing glumly at a dingy outline drawing labelled '*kelev*, a dog'. My other principal memory is of a teacher who had broken one of the loops of the braces holding up his trousers, and replaced it with a piece of string. I wasn't sorry when I stopped going there. (As far as I know the whole scheme came to an end.)

Meanwhile, I had acquired a little collection, no more than four or five books, of Bible stories retold for children. Old Testament stories, I need hardly say. One volume, much scribbled over, was published by a local Jewish publisher in the East End; the others, each with a few colour plates of patriarchs and prophets dressed in robes striped like deckchairs, could just as well have been Sunday school prizes. Either way, the stories themselves worked their spell. Moses in the bulrushes was one particular favourite. Another, less accountably, was Naaman the Syrian being cured of leprosy. My fancy was caught by the names Abana and Pharpar, the 'rivers of Damascus' which the poor man had thought would be as effective in healing him as the waters of the Jordan.

When I was six or seven the stories and the language in which they had been written began to come together for me, just a little. My father remained working in London throughout the war. But after a time he was able to spend odd days with us, usually at the weekend. Brief though his visits were, and tired though he must have been, he was determined not to let slip the chance to teach me some of the elements of Judaism – to pass on the torch, in however guttering or spluttering a condition. We began at the beginning, *in* the beginning, with the first chapter of Genesis, translating it phrase by phrase. We moved forward in a slow, irregular fashion, with a certain amount of memorising and a good deal of skipping, repetition, moving around. Sometimes we began a session by retracing our steps, sometimes we jumped forward from the middle of one section or *'sedra'* – if that was where we had broken off last time – to the start of the next. I don't know whether there was a master plan, but in the event we never got further than the early chapters of Exodus.

It was all very scrappy and limited, but I don't think it could have been called superficial – not, at least, in its imaginative impact. The characters I read about were not merely as real to me as Ali Baba or Robin Hood, they were *really* real – all this had once taken place – and they were the more real for my feeling personally linked to them: they were the founders of the family. This didn't mean, of course, that they weren't also exotic and larger than life. Sarah eavesdropping at the door of the tent, Jacob wrestling with the angel, Moses striking down the Egyptian taskmaster: the pictures of them which took shape in my mind were at once intimate and remote. Sometimes they were pictures formed with very little to go on. All I knew about Padan-Aram was that it was the home of Laban, but the ground there seemed as firm underfoot as though I were there myself. At other times private associations came into play. God's promise to Abraham – 'I will multiply thy seed as the stars of the heaven, and as the sand which is upon the sea-shore' – summoned up a persistent image not only of sea and stars, but also of clumps of grass in the foreground, ruffled by the breeze. Perhaps I had been wondering exactly what 'seed' was, and got it mixed up with the idea of grass-seed.

Contact with Hebrew made my impressions more intense. Judged by ordinary standards, I picked up only a smattering of the language, but individual terms and phrases became invested with a power which makes 'smattering' not quite the right word. After a time, for example, *ha-shomayim* – heaven – came to seem the thing itself, and 'heaven' no more than a pale approximation. Other words felt entirely natural from the first, as though I had always known them. Yet others struck with such hammer-like force that it was impossible to forget them after a single encounter. *Lech lecha*, for instance, 'get thee out': the title and opening words of the third *sedra* of Genesis, God's original injunction to Abraham. (My father hardly ever tested me on what we had read, but until I had mastered them he used to make me run through the titles of the *sedras*, which were often verbs, and easy to confuse *Vayyera*, *Vayyetze*, *Vayyishlach*, *Vayyigash* . . . 'And he appeared', 'And he went out', 'And he sent', 'And he drew near' . . .)

As for the stories themselves, in almost every case I simply accepted them. Looking back, I realise that my father made it easier for me by skating over the harsher episodes and emphasising the more benign or forgiving ones. Reading about Noah, we dwelled on the building of the ark (I wondered what gopher wood was), on the dove, on the rainbow covenant. In the story of Sodom and Gomorrah, it was Abraham's pleading which was underlined – 'Shall not the Judge of all the earth act justly?' – rather than the destruction of the cities itself. But there was one episode, the sacrifice of Isaac, which was too stark to ignore, and against which even a small child might be moved to protest.

In Hebrew the sacrifice is known as the *akedah*, the binding. This is strictly speaking more accurate, since when it comes to it, Isaac is spared. But the binding seemed to me bad enough. What kind of God was it who commanded a father to kill his son? What kind of father was it who was ready to obey? What kind of son was it who meekly aquiesced? The thing was a great scandal. Possibly I found it all the more disturbing because my father's name was Abraham. And there was a grim exclusive masculinity about the whole transaction. Where was Sarah? What did she say when she first heard what the men had been up to?

I can't recall whether I questioned my father about the story, but

I know that it raised doubts, as nothing else in the Bible did at the time – and as it surely always must. Certainly none of the attempts to explain it which I have read in later life have made it acceptable. The best that can be said is that the cruelty lies in the test rather than in its outcome. After it is over, Genesis resumes its normal flow, with its emphasis on transmission, continuity, procreation: within a chapter or two Isaac is marrying Rebecca. But the chasm has opened up, however briefly, and the lesson seems clear. Faith itself is a form of binding (and indeed the word 'religion', which comes from the Latin *ligare*, to bind, implies as much). If God confers freedom, it is on His own terms; potentially His demands are absolute.

I mustn't give the impression that I fretted over the binding of Isaac at the expense of everything else. It was only an episode, more like a jolt; I was still held by the other stories, above all by the superb cycle of stories about Joseph.

Among its other attractions, the Joseph narrative offered a measure of emotional compensation to anyone who had been chilled by the earlier tale. Jacob refusing to be comforted for the death (as he supposed) of Joseph stood out in healthy contrast to the docility of Abraham, while I don't think any verse in those early Bible lessons moved me more than his cry at the thought of losing Benjamin as well: 'you will bring down my grey hairs with sorrow to the grave.' *That* was how a father ought to lament the loss, or prospective loss, of a son – with a full heart.

The most striking thing about the story of Joseph, however, was that it was a success story. Cast into the pit, sold into slavery, he had none the less made it to the top, as his dreams had promised him he would; made it to the top, moreover, in the big non-Jewish world. There was stuff here for the imagination to feed on. There were also complications. Joseph was brilliant, but hadn't he been asking for trouble? Even a child could see that this success story was also a story which began with tale-bearing, favouritism, provocation. And wasn't there something not quite right, even to a child, about the cat-and-mouse game that he played with his brothers later on, before he was ready to forgive them? Yet a success story it remained, in its essential outline, right to the end.

The translation we used was in language quite close to that of the Authorised Version. (It had originally been prepared, I believe, by the Jewish Publication Society of America.) My father also read me many of the later Bible stories in English. My favourite – let psychologists make of it what they will – was the story of David and Absalom. I can recall asking to hear it all over again, as soon as my father had finished: I had a clear picture of the handsome rebellious prince, fleeing from David's victorious army, caught by his hair in the branches of a tree.

Meanwhile, my sense of the singularity of being Jewish was heightened by the fact that our Jewishness found very little expression at this time outside the home. We were separated from the extended world of cousins and uncles and aunts; we had few contacts with other Jews; we lived in a town without a synagogue. Under the circumstances, various minor traditions were abandoned even earlier than they might otherwise have been. I have a dim memory, for example, dating from the age of four or five, of playing with a *dreidl*, a kind of spinning top decorated with Hebrew letters which is used in a children's game during the festival of Chanukah. The experience wasn't repeated. But then it was only a sideshow, so to speak. The main symbol of Chanukah, a menorah (an eight-branched candlestick), stood on a mantelpiece. When the week-long festival came round, the candles were duly lit, an extra one each day; in time, too, I learned to sing the rousing Chanukah song *Ma'oz Tzur* ('Fortress and Rock'). I couldn't have translated much of it without the aid of the crib on the facing page, but some of its words had a wonderful ring to them, the proper names in particular: I rejoiced in the succulent syllables of Zerubovel (Zerubbabel, rebuilder of the temple) and Agagi ben Hamdossa (the Agagite, son of Hamedatha – a roundabout way of referring to Haman, the deadly enemy of the Jews in the Book of Esther).

The nearest synagogue services were in Staines, a much bigger, more cityfied place than Egham, a mile or two across the river. (Staines was in Middlesex, Egham was in Surrey.) We generally managed to get to them for the major festivals; but even in Staines there was no permanent synagogue at the time, and the services were held in borrowed premises, school halls and the like, fusty surroundings which did little to lift my spirit. I was often bored, too, by the proceedings themselves. Only at a few points was my attention completely held – above all by the blowing of the shofar, or ram's horn. Something of the solemnity of the ceremony was borne in upon me, though even here I was partly intrigued (and as I looked around I could see that I wasn't alone) by what you might call its purely human aspects. The shofar has three distinct notes, played in a strict sequence, and producing them is a task which calls for considerable skill. Sometimes the performer would get stuck at the beginning of a note, like a car which was having trouble getting started, and there was a subversive thrill in wondering whether he was going to make it – just as there was in wondering whether he would have enough breath left for the sustained final blast, the *tekiah gedolah*. But I still felt relief when he succeeded (as he somehow always did), and found it satisfying to join in the surge of communal congratulation.

Among my memories of the pilgrimages to Staines, one incident stands out. The Kol Nidre service, on the eve of the Day of Atonement, had finished, and my father and I were setting out on the long walk home through the dark. (I am fairly sure that the year was 1944.) As we turned on to Staines Bridge, we saw a couple of American airmen coming towards us, making a lot of noise and obviously drunk. We crossed the road – there was nobody else about – and once we had got past them my father remarked, 'Well, let's not forget' (or words to that effect) 'that they're made in the image of God.' I am certain that he wasn't being ironic; and what strikes me most, looking back, is that I find it hard to imagine anyone I know today (myself very much included) making such a comment *without* being ironic. If we did try to talk like that, it would sound embarrassing, even unctuous. But it was another time, and the words seemed entirely natural.

In the war years I occasionally caught glimpses of real, fully-fledged synagogues during visits to London. The first one I got to know well, however, was in Cambridge, where I was packed off to school in 1946 – to the Perse, a day school with a couple of houses for boarders, one of them Jewish. (It was known as Hillel House.) The Cambridge synagogue was bright, compact, enlivened by the presence of undergraduates; the services there seldom seemed oppressive, and though my thoughts still strayed, it wasn't necessarily very far. When time hung heavy I often turned to 'Ethics of the Fathers', a collection of ancient rabbinic sayings reprinted in the prayer book. A few of them seemed repetitious, a few of them remote – and I would have been more comfortable, childish though the thought was, if one of the sages who were cited had had a less odd-sounding name than Ben Bag-Bag. But for the most part I was impressed, even stirred.

'Ethics of the Fathers' (they are known as *Pirkei Oves*, 'Chapters of the Fathers', in Hebrew) is a name first applied to the collection by Christian scholars, which is one gauge of the breadth of its appeal. On the other hand one of the very few times I heard my father complain about his upbringing back in Poland was when he recalled the custom of making children study *Pirkei Oves* (he used the popular name *Perek*) on Sabbath afternoons. One particular occasion still rankled. It had been summer, and he had been longing to play outside; instead he had found himself stuck in class, forced to go through a grim passage about graves and worms. Ancestral wisdom, it was clear, had several different faces.

Hillel House provided a certain amount of religious instruction. The outside teacher who had been hired for the purpose, Dr Margolis – instantly nicknamed 'Moggy' – was an elderly man with a fleshy nose and a small neat iron-grey beard. Until the *Anschluss* he had been the rabbi of a large provincial community in Austria: he was a sad figure, and if we had known his full story he would probably have seemed sadder still. For schoolboys, however, the main thing about him (as his pussycat nickname implied) was that he was someone from whom they had nothing to fear. He was also, perhaps not coincidentally, a fairly hopeless teacher. But who can tell what is going to remain from childhood? When a thousand competent lessons from other teachers have been forgotten, I can still remember him breaking off one day and trying to tell us, in his heavily accented English, about a film he had just seen, Vittorio De Sica's *Shoeshine*. It was startling (until then I had hardly connected him with the ordinary world where people went to the cinema). I also found it rather moving; I still do.

As my thirteenth birthday approached, it was Dr Margolis who was entrusted with preparing me for my bar mitzvah. The ceremony involved my being 'called up' in synagogue to read a portion from that week's section of the Torah (the Pentateuch), and an additional passage from the Prophets; it wasn't only the words which had to be mastered, but the correct manner in which they were meant to be chanted.

The Sabbath in question was a special one, and the readings, commemorating the war between the Israelites and the Amalekites, were exceptionally ferocious. Having failed to allow for the complexities of the Jewish calendar, however, Dr Margolis set about teaching me the wrong material. When his mistake was discovered, there were only a few days in hand. But my father somehow got in touch with an undergraduate, a law student from Liverpool, and asked him whether he would take over – which he did, with impressive efficiency. So everything ended happily, with me saying (or singing) my piece, piping away, exhorting the congregation to remember Amalek and smite him utterly.

Not long afterwards I left the Perse, moved to a new school, the City of London, and rejoined my family in Mile End. The local synagogue, which I had already got to know during the holidays, and which was soon to become the one I knew best, was in a quiet turning off Bow Road called Harley Grove. It was affiliated to the United Synagogue – the 'Established Church' of Anglo-Jewry, and an organisation with strong anglicising tendencies; but it would have been hard to think of it as anything but a *shul*, even so. In those first years after the war, it still had a flavour of the old immigrant East End. There were still elderly men there who prayed with prayer shawls over their heads. The rabbi, Rabbi Lew, was not only foreign-born, he still gave sermons in Yiddish (though fewer and fewer of his congregation can have understood them with every year that passed).

Thinking of Harley Grove today, I recall first of all faces. Homely faces, with a family resemblance; lined faces; animated faces; shrewd faces; foolish faces; Jewish faces. Blurred faces, most of them, though a few still stand out sharply. There were the two men who sat immediately behind me, for instance. One, Konopinski, had a tough, humorous, self-contained look, and no doubt he had needed all those qualities in his time: he had got out of Poland at the beginning of the war and served with the Polish army in exile. The other, as though to illustrate how different Jews could be from one another, even within the same small congregation, was an unmistakable Londoner, and far from self-contained: he had a thunderous singing voice, which he used to particularly deafening effect in the hymn *Ein Kelohenu* ('There is none like our God').

The face I remember most clearly is that of someone with whom I never exchanged a word, and of whom I knew nothing except in his public role – Levy the *shammes* (*shammes* being a word variously translated as 'sexton', 'beadle' and 'usher'). He was a very small man with ferrety features, and a uniform consisting of black gown and top hat which made him look like something out of Daumier. He used to scuttle around, reprimanding people who were talking too much, or gathering up discarded prayer books, but his great moments came when he had to make announcements. I can hear him now, proclaiming the time at which the following week's Sabbath began (except that it never began, it always 'commenced'), or at which the following day's service ended (except that it always 'terminated').

Rabbi Lew naturally commanded more respect in my eyes, partly *ex officio*, partly because he spoke out of an immemorial past. But his foreignness could also make him seem quaint. There was an especially unholy joy in hearing him read the prayer for the royal family (the only part of the service in English) and intercede with the Almighty on behalf of 'Her suffering lot Kins Odds' – our sovereign lord King George – and 'Her creche is Quin Hell is a butt', to say nothing of 'May rid a Quin Mudder'. (I have borrowed these transliterations from a letter which once appeared in the *Jewish Chronicle* giving a phonetic version of the entire prayer as it used to be read out by an older generation of East End rabbis. It struck me as pretty accurate.)

The rabbi's remoteness was somewhat diminished by the fact that he was a friend of my father, and that he and his family (he had a multitude of children) were all patients. He would sometimes drop by to see my parents, especially in the early days of their marriage, and one small episode made a lasting impression – on my mother, at least; she recounted it to me with amusement long after my father's death. My parents had bought an art deco statuette (much admired by me as a child) of a naked sylph or goddess perched on a green malachite base. One day not long afterwards the rabbi showed up unannounced, and just before he came into the room my father, in a desperate move, hung his hat over the graceful but offending object. A friend was a friend, and a patient was a patient, but a rabbi was still a rabbi.

Rabbi Lew's successors gave their sermons in English. There was a good deal of nagging in them, about the lax observance of religious laws; there were warnings against 'ostentation' and appeals for 'decorum'. This last was a favourite theme, although the relative lack of decorum was in fact one of the *shul*'s more attractive features. It shouldn't be exaggerated (things never got *that* far out of hand), but there was something reassuringly sociable about the pockets of independent activity, the *sotto voce* conversations, the way in which people constantly seemed to be wandering in and out.

If there were slack periods during services, there were also times of dedication and intensity. The atmosphere during Kol Nidre, the evening service at the start of the fast of Yom Kippur (the Day of Atonement), was particularly charged – so much so that something like a secondary ritual developed. Almost every year (at least, it seemed like that), not long into the service, there would be a sensation up in the ladies' gallery. An old lady would faint, and my father would be summoned from downstairs, amid much clucking and scuffling, to make sure that she was all right.

My own commitment to the acts of worship in which I was supposed to be taking part had its limits. I was still frequently bored; there was a great deal I didn't understand; I often lost my place. And in a more general way, I never felt quite at home. I had always known that the synagogue could never be *the* centre of my world, simply *a* centre. But was it even as much as that?

There is a brilliant account of an estranged Jewish child in synagogue in Franz Kafka's celebrated 'Letter to His Father'. When I first read it, twenty or thirty years after the period I am describing, I had moved on, but the past was still dear to me, and I felt an immediate sense of constriction round my heart. Kafka paints an unsparing picture of the tedium he endured when he attended services with his father (he says that the only time he was ever again so bored was at dancing lessons!); he recalls his alienation, his moments of outright distaste, his dread that he would one day find himself 'called up' to read a portion of the Torah. And what he said not only rang true, it was also enormously recognisable. Hence my distress. He made me suspect that this was what I had really felt myself, and that my boyhood devotions – if one was going to be honest – had never been anything more than a dutiful sham.

I reminded myself that he was writing out of a different situation; that he had been driven by animus against his father; that his bitterest complaint was that his father's Judaism had been formal and inauthentic, which was something I could never have said about my own father, and which might possibly have been unfair in *his* case, too. But I still felt oppressed.

It was a single macabre image which broke the spell. Recalling how he would try to alleviate his boredom in the synagogue by clutching at such 'few little bits of variety as there were', Kafka instances the moment at which the Ark of the Covenant was opened and the Scrolls of the Law brought out. He compares it to the cupboard door in a shooting gallery which opened whenever one scored a bull's-eye – with the difference that 'there something interesting always came out, and here it was always just the same old dolls with no heads'.

A compelling image, certainly. Pure expressionism; it makes the Ark sound like a second cabinet of Dr Caligari. But when I reread the passage, and thought about it, I knew, simply *knew*, that it didn't tally with my own experience. The bringing out of the Scrolls from the Ark and the returning of them after the reading were always high points for me. I may not often have been among the men who pressed forward to kiss them as they were carried past (to kiss them at one remove, by touching them with a prayer shawl and then holding the shawl to one's lips). But I shared at least some of the emotion I felt being poured out around me, just as I found myself caught up in the accompanying singing. As for the Scrolls themselves, I could never have thought of them as dolls, or anything like dolls, even at my most detached; and the idea of them as headless dolls – not merely toys, but broken toys – was even more fantastic. On the contrary, they seemed wonderfully intact and complete, all the more so when one considered the immense care which had gone into preparing them, the absolute necessity of the scribe getting every letter right. They were what they were; mutilation, except in a bad dream, was inconceivable.

In the end Kafka acted as a challenge. If he forced me to admit that much of my early religious experience (more of it than I would have been willing to admit before) was pseudo-experience, dead wood, he also stung me into protesting, once I had recovered myself, that some of it had been genuine. And this in turn unlocked memories – of forgotten intensities, of the moments in a service which I had known could be relied on to touch the heart.

One such moment was the beautiful Friday night hymn *Lecha dodi*, 'Come, my friend', with its invitation to welcome the Sabbath as a bride. Another was *U'nsana tokef*, the great tremulous prayer recited on the Day of Atonement, with its image of mankind passing before God on the Day of Judgment like a flock of sheep passing before a shepherd. *Lecha dodi* made the joy of religion palpable; *U'nsana tokef* was enough in itself to explain why the High Festivals are known in Hebrew as *Yomim noraim*, the days of awe.

A year or two ago I read an article in a magazine which set me thinking about Kafka and his headless dolls once again.

The Ark is the focal point of a synagogue. It is set in the eastern wall and covered with embroidered curtains: to a believer it can easily seem to contain mysterious depths. But as soon as it is demystified, looked at with a cold eye, it becomes nothing more than what Kafka called it, a cupboard.

The article I have mentioned was an account of a nostalgic visit to Whitechapel, and more particularly to a room which had once served as a tiny immigrant *shul*. The premises now belonged to an Indian textile merchant, but inside, among the bolts and lengths of cloth, the cupboard which had once been the Ark was still plain to see. Observing the author's interest, the owner told him: 'We know it was something special, so we only use it for storing our very best material.'

The last time I visited Harley Grove, incidentally, I found that the synagogue is now a Sikh temple. I didn't attempt to go inside, but I couldn't help wondering about the young people who worship there, and about how far they feel torn between the claims of the past and the constant pressures of acculturation. Not, I suppose, that 'acculturation' is the word they actually use, any more than it was the word we used fifty years ago.

3

Jewishness

Judaism has many shades. My family belonged to the category which I believe sociologists of religion call 'residual Orthodox'. They were consistently observant in some respects (they would never have considered eating non-kosher food, for instance), fitfully observant in others (they remembered the Sabbath day and kept it holy, up to a point) and completely relaxed about ignoring a whole mass of lesser regulations.

In the eyes of the truly Orthodox they would, of course, have been marked down as backsliders, but I don't think this would have distressed them unduly. When they referred to someone as *frum*, strictly Orthodox, the implication (unless he was a rabbi or an old-timer) tended to be not so much that he deserved extra respect as that he was rigid, pedantic, a bit out of it. Beyond the strictly Orthodox lay the even less congenial territory of the ultra-Orthodox, while as for the bearded and black-garbed Hassidim – seldom seen in the East End, but a growing presence in Stamford Hill and some of the other areas to the north – the sense of their outlandishness was sufficiently signalled by the fact that the nickname we used for them was 'Peruvians'. (Poor Peru.) And yet the residue in our residual Orthodoxy meant a great deal to us. I can't imagine anyone in the immediate family belonging to a congregation which wasn't Orthodox at least in principle. Reform and Liberal synagogues were out of bounds.

This middle way – traditional without being fundamentalist, observant but not too much – probably represented the position of the majority of British Jews at the time. It was a comfortable compromise; certainly in my own case it helped to stave off what would otherwise have been a much sharper questioning of what I was taught. For, from an early age, there were passages in the Bible (and elsewhere) which, if I had been required to take them literally, I would have found morally repellent. As it was, the more problematic aspects of the Old Testament God were either allegorised away or subjected to benign neglect.

The injunction to destroy Amalek, for example: it was a comfort to find no less an authority than the formidable Chief Rabbi of my childhood, J.H. Hertz, explaining that it should be understood as a call 'to blot out from the human heart the cruel Amalek spirit'. I was far from convinced that this had been the intention of whoever wrote the passage, but I didn't doubt that Hertz's comment represented his own deepest conviction – that this was the point in our moral development we were supposed to have reached. All around me, in fact, there was evidence of how much Judaism, for all its continuities, had evolved over the millennia, of how far it had been rendered milder and more humane. The old ferocities hadn't been entirely forgotten. They were still capable, alas, of being reactivated, as extremist groups in Israel and their supporters have shown. But the climate in which I and everyone I knew grew up was temperate. We took it for granted that God's jealousy counted for a good deal less than his mercy and loving kindness.

Yet one question undercut everything else. Religion might express itself through respect for tradition, intensity of feeling, devotion to a way of life. But how much did I actually believe?

I find it hard to recall a time when I didn't wonder whether the whole thing simply wasn't true. Where was the evidence? And how much evidence seemed to point the other way! In due course my doubts increased, fed partly by reading, partly by reflection. I had no inclination to argue about faith (perhaps because I was afraid that religion would always lose the argument). Either you believed or you didn't. But though I did my best to hive it off, my scepticism continued to grow.

Being Jewish hardly began and ended with religious belief, however. It entailed a whole complex of other considerations as well – loyalties, affinities, cultural legacies, folkways, habits of mind. It involved difficult choices, and issues where the choice was out of one's hands.

For Jews from Eastern Europe, the most obvious extension of their religion was the much-invoked concept of *Yiddishkeit*, 'Jewishness' – a way of life which coexisted with religion, but which was capable to some extent of surviving it; and no feature of *Yiddishkeit* was more central than a knowledge of the Yiddish language itself. Among the children of immigrants, that knowledge inevitably thinned out. By the third generation, it had generally been reduced to a scattering of words and phrases. But the fragments still had life in them. They remained embedded in everyday talk.

Of the hundreds of Yiddish words which I heard as a child, the most indispensable were those with a specifically Jewish meaning – religious terms, for the most part, although food contributed a substantial number as well. In principle, they could have been translated, but nobody I knew would have dreamed of talking about a cantor rather than a *chazan*, any more than they would have talked about noodles rather than *lokshen*. Praying was *davnen* (or more likely, *davening*, since verbs used in isolation tended to be conjugated as though we were speaking English). *Leynen* was to read aloud from the Torah, *bentshn* was to say grace. A *rebbitsin* was not simply a rabbi's wife, but as much a public figure in her own right as, shall we say, a mayoress.

Beyond this inner-core vocabulary there were general terms which could theoretically be used in a non-Jewish context, but which almost always carried a Jewish connotation in practice. A *shnayder* was emphatically a Jewish tailor, not the kind you expected to find in Savile Row. Finally, and most extensively, there were all the words and phrases which had been retained because they were felt to be particularly expressive, or unmistakably 'right', or simply too intimate a link with the past to be readily parted with. No pleasure, or so it seemed, could be quite as acute as a *mechaye*, no troubles weighed quite as heavily as *tsores*. *Rachmones* was the deepest form of pity. There was a certain mood of sulkiness for which only *broyges* would do.

Most of the Yiddish words used at home were drawn from the common stock of what might be called 'Anglo-Yiddish': they would have been familiar to anyone from a similar background. A few, on the other hand, were terms which bubbled up under pressure, and which I can recall hearing my father use only once – when he was moved to describe a particularly rascally character as a *ferdganef* (a horse-thief), for instance. And then there were favourite expressions which he would quote or explain rather than actually use. One such example was *kochlefl*, a cooking spoon – purely Germanic in origin, but used colloquially in Yiddish to mean a busybody, a spoon for stirring things round and stirring them up. Another phrase which he once cited – not his personal style, I would have thought, but he recalled it with a smile – was a very Yiddish way of saying that something was not too bad and not too good: *s'iz nit oy-oy-oy un nit ay-ay-ay.*

I couldn't help noticing that some of the most cherished of these favourite phrases turned on the themes of false or inadequate piety. A *tsadik in peltz*, 'a righteous man in furs', was a play on words. *Tsadik* not only signified righteousness or even saintliness; it was also (very nearly) the name of the last letter – a mere letter, nothing more – in the word *pelts*. *Frim vi der alter Maksim* 'as observant or devout as old Maxim', meant not observant at all. It made fun of a regional pronunciation, *frim* instead of *frum*, and linked it by means of a mocking rhyme with the name of an archetypal Russian peasant.

Locutions like these were echoes of an already fast vanishing past. Even for my father, their principal appeal lay in their quaintness. But there were other, more familiar Yiddish terms which were still applied with their full force – which were meant to instil values. There were the words which encouraged you, if one can say such a thing, to be intelligent, not to be a *schlemiel*. There were the words which counselled generosity, large-mindedness, *mentschlichkeit*. There were, not least, the words which presupposed a decent standard of manners. *Grob* (coarse) and *prost* (crude, utterly common) were terms of censure which I frequently heard; a *grober yung* (a coarse young man, a lout) was a very undesirable creature indeed. And anyone who supposes that coarseness and crudeness weren't realities to be contended with would be deluding himself, as no one but a *schlemiel* would ever have deluded himself in the shtetl or the East End. How could it have been otherwise? Social and economic conditions had been discouraging, often harsh, for hundreds of years. The impressive thing is how determined an effort there had been, in the face of them, to maintain an ideal of refinement and sensitivity.

This is putting matters too simply, however. Yiddish is a very down-to-earth language. Its slang is pungent; its proverbs often have a rough edge; it makes ample allowance for the less elevated aspects of human nature. It is also a language rich in insults and curses, of which it is hard to imagine even the most refined speaker not availing himself from time to time. My father was, in most respects, a mild man, but he would none the less occasionally let slip – simply by way of an expletive, I need hardly add – a standard Yiddish curse: *Khob im in drerd*, for instance ('I have him in the earth', he can go to hell) or *a kholyera oyf im* ('a cholera on him', with the stress on the middle syllable of *kholyera*, which made it sound all the more vehement). He was also, I would say, an unusually polite man, but in private he would sometimes have recourse to some fairly basic Yiddish (never English) to relieve his feelings. One of his tricks, when he had been talking to a particularly tiresome acquaintance, was to make his farewells and then murmur *kish mir 'n tuches* ('kiss my arse'). He was living dangerously, too: the other person was sometimes barely out of earshot.

At the same time he would have been horrified if anyone had identified the spirit of Yiddish with its vulgarisms, or with a few 'cute' phrases torn out of context. He was anxious to let me know that it was a language as good as any other; that it had its eloquence, its seriousness, its variety, its heights as well as its depths. Part of his concern was that I shouldn't be misled by the cheap sprinklings of Yiddish used by comedians and the like. But he was also protesting against the low status of a language which he was used to hearing spoken of with condescension or disdain. To some extent, I think, he was reliving the arguments of the period during which he had grown up, in which Yiddish was regularly assailed by its opponents within the East European Jewish world – modernisers, Hebraists and others – as a mere 'jargon'. 'They called it *zhargon*,' he explained to me more than once. The insult still stung.

Yet how much stake did I really have in a language which I could neither speak nor, for the most part, understand? Kafka, whose engagement with his Jewishness didn't end – in some respects only began – with his disaffection from the synagogue, once told a Jewish audience in Prague, 'I assure you, ladies and gentlemen, that you understand far more Yiddish than you think.' In the 1950s Irving Howe quoted this sentence at the outset of his path-breaking anthology of Yiddish stories in translation, and it has often been quoted since: the idea is a flattering one (especially if we choose to overlook the fact that Kafka was speaking in German, which is of course far closer to Yiddish than English). But like other instances of flattery, it can be misleading. If you want to appreciate a language properly, there is no substitute for learning it – which is what I should have done, at some stage, if I had cared enough. I didn't.

It is a narrow purism which would leave the matter there, however, and it would be as wrong to deny the significance of the last scraps of inherited Yiddish as it would be to make too much of them. A little learning, in the right context, can exert a powerful hold; a feeling at one remove may be only a shadow of the original, but it is still a lot sharper than a feeling at ten removes. To Yiddish speakers, Yiddish was *mame-loshn*, the mother tongue – a term so warm and intimate that it almost sounds like a diminutive. To their English-speaking children and grandchildren, it could never be that; but something of the warmth and intimacy could still be glimpsed and even shared.

One way of getting closer to Yiddish would naturally have been through its literature. I read one or two classics in childhood – some of Sholem Aleichem's tales of his fictitious small town Kasrilevke, Isaac Loeb Peretz's inescapable story of the simple-hearted Bontshe Schweig – but few good translations or attractive editions were available. It was only around 1960 that the treasures began to be unlocked, in books from America – Irving Howe's anthologies (of verse and non-fiction as well as fiction), the reissues of Maurice Samuel's brilliant interpretive studies of Sholem Aleichem and Peretz, high-level translations such as Saul Bellow's version of Isaac Bashevis Singer's *Gimpel the Fool*.*

* Since Singer has become far and away the best-known modern Yiddish writer

34

My father himself read little Yiddish writing in the years when I was growing up. This was no doubt largely due to the pressures and disruptions of the time, and the pressures of his own work, though I feel sure things would have been rather different if he had been in America, where Yiddish was so very much more alive. As it is, collective Yiddish culture in London was fading fast. The last Yiddish daily paper, for example, *Di Tsayt*, closed down in 1950, and long before that it had become an established joke that whenever the editor, Morris Myer, saw a Jewish funeral cortège making its way down Whitechapel Road, he used to say, 'There goes another subscriber.' *Di Tsayt* had a successor, which my father occasionally brought home, called *Di Yidishe Shtimme*, the Jewish Voice; but by this time, alas, the voice was a faint one. It came out once a week.

Yet within this shrinking world some kind of literary life still went on. There were a small group of writers who banded together – one of their favourite hangouts was a Lyons tea shop across the road from the London Hospital – and who organised readings and recitals. Some of them had been well-known East End figures in their day. B.A. Sokhatchevski, for instance, was a veteran journalist, though I later learned that he had also published large quantities of verse (sad verse, much of it, about a son who died at the age of twelve). L.S. Kreditor was a journalist of even longer standing – and the father-in-law of Hugh Gaitskell. But the dominant personality of the group was undoubtedly the poet A.N. Stencl, founder and mainstay of the magazine *Loshn un Lebn* ('Language and Life').

There was only one Stencl. He was probably only a minor poet, but I don't think anyone who met him could ever have doubted

---

in the world at large, I can't resist pointing out that there are others worth reading. At least one of them, the poet and storyteller Jacob Glatstein, has in fact moved me and got through to me in a way Singer never quite has: his poems about the Holocaust in particular are the most adequate (or least inadequate) I know. It is hard to believe that if Glatstein had written in English he wouldn't be regarded as a major figure. He lived in New York, and Irving Howe once heard him complain, 'The thing about being a Yiddish poet is that I have to know about Auden but Auden doesn't have to know about me.'

that he was a true poet. He lived in a small council flat in Whitechapel, but I sometimes saw him standing at the back of Jewish meetings in central London or the West End, waiting to hawk a copy or two of *Loshn un Lebn* when the audience dispersed. He was a handsome man, somewhat Spanish in appearance, I thought. We never exchanged more than a word of greeting and a smile, but his smile was worth having: it was one of those smiles that seem to say, 'What, finally, can we do? But we must do what we can.'

It was only after his death that I learned some of the main facts of his career. He came from a well-known family of rabbis; his father was head of the rabbinical court in the Polish city of Czestochowa (famous among Christians as a place of pilgrimage and the home of the 'Black Virgin'). He himself had begun as a yeshiva student, but he had left home in 1919 and led a bohemian life in Holland and then Germany: his first poems were published in Leipzig and Berlin. After Hitler came to power he moved to London, and from the outset he seems to have been determined to see the East End not just as a refuge but as his home. Scanning the list of his publications in Leonard Prager's invaluable *Yiddish Culture in London*, I find something immeasurably touching at the thought of him in the late thirties, with the storm clouds gathering, bringing out a little booklet entitled *Sof-zumer ferzn in a vayttshepl gesl*, 'Late Summer Verses in a Whitechapel Lane'. And he was to remain loyal to Whitechapel, or to his ideal conception of Whitechapel, to the very end, both in his writings and in his way of life.

When my father died, Stencl published an editorial paragraph in his memory in *Loshn un Lebn*. The two men had been friends, and on at least one occasion my father had turned to him for literary advice. During my last term at school, with plenty of leisure, I set about working my way through Scott Moncrieff's Proust. My father (though he didn't tell me until afterwards) wondered whether it was wise for me to devote quite so much time to a single author, especially an author he had never heard of. He asked Stencl what he thought, and the poet's immediate response was abrupt and unexpected, but reassuring: 'Better than Thomas Mann.'

There was one other contemporary or near-contemporary Yiddish writer whom my father mentioned once or twice, and whom he had clearly been impressed by – a Polish-Jewish essayist and journalist called Hillel Zeitlin. I was mildly intrigued, not least because I never seemed to come across his name anywhere else. Eventually, I was to find out something about him; but that belongs to a later stage of the story.

Jewishness spilled out from its original religious core in many directions. Sometimes secular pleasure and sacred uplift overlapped – in the work of the great *chazanim* or cantors, for instance, the stars of their profession like Sirota and Rosenblatt who went on tour and who were capable of filling large concert halls. (They were only names to me when I was a boy; later on, their recordings began to be reissued on LP and cassette.) At the other extreme, there were political groups – both Zionist and (in those days) socialist – which were often aggressively anti-religious, but which still defined themselves as Jewish by race or culture. In between came a mass of social institutions which generally had a formal religious aspect, but which also had a life of their own, in which religion played no more than a marginal role. And then – harder to measure, and subject to endless variations – there were common attitudes, activities and personal characteristics.

Names, which always fascinated me, were one of the great distinguishing marks. I can't recall a time when it didn't seem fairly obvious which surnames were Jewish and which were not. Drucker, Spiro, Nussbaum, Sacks, Warshafsky, Unger, Weinstock, Frumkin, Lipman, Segal . . . Family names, the neighbours' names and the names of my father's patients all combined to impress the difference on me. A few names caught my fancy by their oddity: I was intrigued by what seemed to be the stammering repetition in the middle of 'Rappaport'. Early on, too, I learned a number of distinctions. Kohn, unlike Cohen, was a German-Jewish name; the Montanges, unlike their neighbours the Perlmutters, were Sephardim. But for the most part the fact that a name was Jewish was simply absorbed, without further thought.

There was one big complication. Between the wars, Jews had begun to change their names with increasing frequency. The inducements were powerful. A Jewish name was not merely, in many quarters, a potential embarrassment; the Nazis had shown that it could also be a dangerous stigma. What is striking, under the circumstances, is how few name-changes there were. No doubt many Jews never got round to considering the option, but for others, rejecting it must have been a question of self-respect. And at least some must have been deterred by the thought of possible criticism. Changing a name could be an embarrassment, too. There were lots of jokes about it.

Still, many Jews did rename themselves – though when they did, they often drew on the same limited stock of new surnames, as though they didn't want the change to go too far. Not always: I had one acquaintance called Abrahams who suddenly reappeared as Addison. But more typically, names like Conway and Ross and Stone and Gould came round again and again. The effect was to create something like a secondary tier of Jewish names. There were contexts in which 'Bernard Kaye' or 'Sidney Lewis' (fictitious examples, needless to say) sounded almost as Jewish as Benjamin Cohen or Sam Levine.

First names afforded more variety. By the time I was born traditional Jewish names (unless they were biblical names in common English use, such as David or Judith) had been almost completely abandoned. By and large my Jewish contemporaries had the kind of first names which everyone else had, although there were a few particular favourites – one or two of them not easily accounted for. I have never understood, for example, why so many Jewish boys of roughly my generation, both here and in America, were named Norman. Another fashion in the years I was growing up was for Scottish names, although it wasn't matched by a fashion for Irish or Welsh ones. A Malcolm Greenberg or an Ian Greenberg might easily have been encountered; a Patrick Greenberg or a Llewellyn Greenberg, in my experience, never. (I did have a cousin called Lloyd, however, and at Passover I often studied the features of Lloyd C. Rakusen of Leeds, whose portrait used to adorn the boxes of matzos he manufactured.)

The road which had started in Ur of the Chaldees and passed through Sinai had branched out into some unlikely directions. Anyone who wanted to give an adequate idea of what being

Jewish meant in the London of fifty years ago (or at any time since) would have to take into account the most varied phenomena, some of them quite mundane – shops, schools, restaurants; the diamond bourse in Hatton Garden, the Leo Baeck College, Petticoat Lane; communal personalities, fund-raising appeals, mammoth bar mitzvah parties; taxi drivers, dance-band leaders, academics, chartered accountants; the rag trade, the *haute juiverie*, the annual parade of ex-servicemen; cookery, favourite football teams, journalism, jokes . . .

The jokes were important. Some were fun while they lasted. A few were inspired, some were terrible, many had seen better days. (I have heard it claimed that Cain killed Abel because he got tired of hearing him tell Jewish jokes he knew already.) What most of them offered, apart from the chance of a laugh, were the pleasures of recognition and social cohesion. Jewish traits were mocked; Gentile traits too, sometimes both together – but Jewish traits on the whole. Much of the humour depended on shared experience; and occasionally, in later life, I have seen such humour manifest itself where I wouldn't have expected it, almost as though it were a last affirmation of Jewishness when all else had gone. An eminent biochemist, who as far as I know had long since severed any links he might have had with the Jewish community, once told me that he had hoaxed his colleagues at a conference by reading a paper about a bogus antibiotic called Bobemycin (*bobbe-myseh* being Yiddish for an old wives' tale).

Beyond the jokes themselves lay floating scraps of comic folklore. Some of it was family folklore, some of it public, drawn from the common stock, and it wasn't always easy to tell which. One of my parents' names for a schemer, for instance, or for anyone who preened himself on his artfulness, was 'cunning Isaacs'. Was it a term they had encountered who knows where, and taken a personal fancy to, or had it once been in more general use? (I was reminded of it years later when I came across the German-Jewish term for the same type, a *Schlaumeyer*.) Or again, there is a sentence which seems to swim up from nowhere, except that I know that I'm very small, and that the room is crowded, and that people are laughing: 'Vot do you tink, Mr Fink, ve sell mink coats for nuffink?' Was it an old joke, or something that a family wit had just come up with? We must all surely have comparable oddities which haunt us simply because they are fragments of an otherwise irrecoverable early childhood – verbal dross which has been alchemised into private gold.

Jewish humour was a source of strength, but there came a point at which it could also be rather lowering. It was a reminder, both in its subject matter and its implications, of something borne in on me as soon as I began to develop any kind of critical detachment, and which plenty of other Jews were in any case willing to point out – the sad fact that Jewish life was often narrow, provincial and materialistic. Chaim Weizmann once described the Jews as a great people and a small people. I must admit that on a day-to-day basis, I was more often struck by the smallness. What else, it may be urged, should I have expected – and wouldn't the same have been true of any people? But I craved for something better, especially as religion began to loosen its grip; and I partly found it, around the age of eleven or twelve, by developing an interest in Jewish history.

The first book in the field which captured my imagination was Israel Zangwill's *Dreamers of the Ghetto*. Zangwill had made his name in 1892 with *Children of the Ghetto*, the first novel of any consequence about the Jewish East End. *Dreamers of the Ghetto*, which had followed six years later, was very different: it was a collection of imaginative sketches of Jewish personalities from the sixteenth century (when the original ghetto in Venice was established) to the end of the nineteenth. The figures portrayed included Spinoza, Heine, Lassalle and the Baal Shem Tov, the founder of Hassidism. There was a glimpse of Disraeli; there were memorable accounts of the seventeenth-century pseudo-Messiah Shabbetai Zevi and the footloose eighteenth-century philosopher Solomon Maimon. At first I simply read the book 'for the story', but I soon realised that everyone in it was either a rebel, or a heretic, or – like Maimon, who had made the transition from the Talmud to the Enlightenment, but found peace in neither – a wanderer between two worlds. What I didn't appreciate at the time was that it owed much of its power to Zangwill's own ambivalence. But for the reader, that was only a secondary consideration. The important thing for me was that it brought home, as nothing else I had read up till then, the variety of Jewish history – and it made it clear that the cross-currents were as much part of the story as the main currents.

Once my interest had been roused it was only a step to the writings of Cecil Roth, the doyen of Anglo-Jewish historians at the time. Roth's *Short History of the Jewish People* provided a basic framework. Later on, his histories of the Marranos and the Jews of Italy were to open up fascinating new territory. But initially the book which appealed to me most was *The Jewish Contribution to Civilization*. Today, this survey of artists, scientists and other distinguished figures who happened to be Jewish might well be looked at askance. Roth himself would readily have agreed that many of the individuals he discussed showed little or no interest in their Jewish origins, and that those origins often had no obvious bearing on their work. But the book has to be seen in context. First published in 1938, it was conceived in an atmosphere thick with slanders (by no means all of them emanating from Germany) which portrayed Jews as eternal middlemen, or parasites, or worse. It was a necessary book in its day, and it remains an interesting one. When I picked it up recently, after an interval of fifty years, I was soon hooked all over again.

Roth taught at Oxford, and I sometimes saw him when I was an undergraduate: he and his wife used to keep open house on Saturday afternoons. Meeting him for the first time could be a startling experience. He was a tall man, with thick glasses, lots of teeth, lank black hair parted in the middle (it was often mistaken for a wig) and a spluttery voice: he looked and sounded rather like an actor got up to play some minor loon in a Feydeau farce – a hotel manager, perhaps. But he was always worth listening to (his conversation abounded in what you might call the higher Jewish gossip), and you never knew who you were going to meet under his roof. One Saturday I found myself sitting next to Pierre Mendès-France, who was French prime minister at the time.

There are greater Jewish historians than Roth. Historiography has in any case moved on – though even when I first began to reflect on what I read, I was puzzled by some of the gaps. Why did he pay so little attention, relatively speaking, to the Jews of Eastern Europe? Why did his *History of the Jews in England* break off in the mid-nineteenth century, before the modern community began to take shape? Rightly or wrongly, I suspected an element of snobbery in his concentration on Sephardic themes. Yet I still feel grateful that it was his books rather those of some better balanced but duller historian which came my way when they did. Everything he wrote was infused with character. He had a romantic feeling for his subject. Not least, he set his face against what has been called the 'lachrymose' interpretation of Jewish history, the emphasis on suffering at the expense of everything else. This wasn't an easy attitude to maintain once Nazism was doing its worst, and he understandably chose not to republish one or two of his earlier, more optimistic essays. The assumptions with which he had begun his career in the 1920s had changed, irrevocably. But he still refused to accept that persecution and martyrdom were the defining characteristics of Jewish history. To have done so, indeed, would have amounted to a final surrender to the Nazis. The horrors were inescapable, in earlier centuries no less than our own, but they weren't the only things worth talking about. It was a richer, more positive story that he had to tell.

For many Jews, whatever the larger historical balance sheet, anti-Semitism is the heart of the matter, the only significant reason why they still feel Jewish. For all Jews, inevitably, having to take account of it represents 'the last attachment': discard religion, cut your communal ties, and prejudice is still liable to turn up at the feast. But to have had a religious upbringing at least ensures that in your own mind you are a Jew first, and the object of other people's dislike second. And after that – well, it has been said that to be Jewish is to belong to a club from which no one is allowed to resign. That isn't wholly true (many individual members of the club have slipped quietly away), and it has grown much less true over the past generation. But as a general statement of how things stood fifty years ago, it will serve.

4

A Doctor's Son

There seems never to have been a time when I wasn't strongly aware that my father was a doctor. For the first four or five years of my life, we lived over the surgery. Both patients and family entered through the same front door, and then went their separate ways – into the waiting room on the left or up the stairs straight ahead. Being a doctor's child in a poor neighbourhood could hardly have failed to confer a sense of privilege; the layout of the house could hardly have failed to reinforce it.

For some reason I was fascinated by the brass rapper on the front door. Perhaps it was another symbol of privilege: *we* didn't have to rap when the door was locked, *we* had a key. At all events, when I set out to revisit the surgery after a gap of thirty years (my son had asked to see it), I found that the rapper was one of the few things I remembered. But when we got there, it had gone. The surgery was now a video store, the entire frontage had been remodelled, and where the door had once stood I was confronted with a life-size cut-out of Kevin Costner playing Robin Hood.

In the old days there had been an opaque green window with an inscription painted on it: my father's name and qualifications, and underneath the legend 'Physician and Accoucheur'. As a somewhat older child, that had intrigued me too. *Accoucheur* was such a strange word. In fact, the inscription must have dated back to the 1920s. By the time I was growing up, there was no longer any call for my father's obstetric skills, but when he first set up in practice, it had been all part of the job.

I sometimes used to visit the surgery after hours, when my father

43

was working there alone. I would explore the deserted waiting room, with its prints of the Cries of London ('Cherry Ripe!', 'Sweet Lavender!'), and the tiny partitioned area with its supply of bottles and labels and corks and its faint smell of a Bunsen burner; I would venture into the mysteriously empty spare room at the back, looking out on the sooty little garden which my mother had tried to brighten up by planting Alexandra roses. The consulting room itself had a shabby air, in comparison with the gleaming white doctors' offices which I saw portrayed in advertisements or at the cinema. Once or twice, left alone there, I sneaked a look at the textbooks stacked on top of a filing cabinet. I was no doubt searching for sexual enlightenment, but the only revelation I can recall – it made me shut the book at once – was a colour plate depicting a hideously inflamed eye. I thought of it long afterwards when I first came across the passage in *Middlemarch* where disenchanted Dorothea watches the red drapery in St Peter's spreading itself 'like a disease of the retina'.

I was never much attracted by the idea of 'playing doctors'. (It might have been different if I had had a sister to take the part of Nurse.) But I was thrilled when my father let me listen in through his stethoscope, and I was amused, around the age of five or six, by the games we sometimes played with medical terms. Telling me to 'Say aaaah' or 'Say ninety-nine' usually produced a laugh, while the word 'ipecacuanha' afforded particular pleasure as a kind of junior tongue-twister. (It was the name of a drug used in those days to help people spit things out or bring them up. It is only recently that I looked it up in the dictionary and found that it derives from a South American Indian word meaning 'emetic creeper'.)

That the consulting room was a place to which people brought their anxieties, a place where some people heard the news they most dreaded – these were considerations which didn't mean much to a child. Nor did I fully register the fact that my father had attended hundreds of deathbeds: the idea of death, too vast for daily experience, belonged in some other compartment. I was impressed, however, when he told me that in his experience better-off patients tended to fight harder for life than poor ones (they had more to lose), but that poor families tended to grieve more passionately over a death than the better off (they had less to console them).

Naturally he didn't discuss the details of his work, but I couldn't help picking up odds and ends. There was one memorable occasion, at lunch. He was talking to my mother about a former patient who had become a successful businessman; I was sitting on the other side of the room, and he can't have realised that I was listening – as indeed I barely was, until I caught the phrase '. . . only got one testicle'. (An uncharacteristic confidence for him to have made to my mother, I would have thought, though of course I can't be sure.) At this period this man's name was quite often to be seen on posters and signboards; a few weeks later when we were out in the car we drove past one such sign, and I announced, with complacent twelve-year-old knowingness, 'The man with one testicle.' The result was something like a panic reaction: 'Don't ever say that again. For God's sake, I could get struck off the register,' etc. But it was a unique incident.

We did hear about the humours of the practice – odd characters and the odd things they said. There was the patient who used to proclaim, with a transparency which would have seemed naive even in pre-Freudian times, that he wanted to marry a girl who looked like his mother. My father had long since written him off as a preordained bachelor, until one day he showed up with a fiancée who could have been his mother's double. Then there was the elderly Jewish woman who had been coming in regularly for years to collect a certificate, and who still called it a 'stiff-ticket'. And there was the genial Irish docker who never visited the surgery without presenting my father with a large carton of Benson and Hedges which he had 'somehow' acquired in the course of his work. His generosity almost certainly did its bit in hastening my father's death.

There were other ways I became aware of patients. During the school holidays, when I was older, my father often took me out with him on visits – ostensibly to look after the car, although in reality I think it was more to keep him company. I used to watch him disappear through the front door or up the tenement steps with his scuffed attaché case, and then settle down to a few pages of a book: one busy afternoon I got through the better part of a detective story. Some of the blocks of flats where he had been summoned had a rough reputation, but they never seemed frightening in the way that a modern 'sink' estate is; and in those days a doctor could expect to be treated with respect, even in the roughest quarters. It was a sign of deference that patients almost always addressed my father as 'Doctor'. At the same time, he couldn't have been stand-offish if he had tried, and I like to think they sensed how much he sympathised with them, especially the poorer ones. There were inevitably a few individual trouble-makers, but almost the only general complaint about slum manners I can recall him making was a very mild one. Emerging one day from a visit to a particularly grim-looking tenement, he said: 'You know, one thing I'll never get used to is the way the really little ones swear, babies who have just learned to talk coming out with f— [his abbreviation] just like that.'

Occasionally, a patient would show up at the front door. (This was after the war, when we had left the surgery and moved to a house nearby.) There was a girl called Betty Aarons whose name I often heard mentioned: she suffered cruelly from asthma. I can still remember the scare I got one day when I was alone in the house, answered the bell and found her standing on the doorstep in the throes of a bad attack. I thought she was dying.

In those early post-war years you could still catch glimpses of the past which was supposed to have been left behind – a child with rickets, for example; other children smeared with the purple ointment which meant they had impetigo. But it was predomi-nantly, unmistakably, a time of hope: medical practice was being remodelled by one great change, the advent of the National Health Service, and transformed by another, the use of antibiotics. My parents strongly supported the idea of the NHS (though without expecting miracles), and I automatically assumed that it was a Good Thing. I also enjoyed the fact that doctors were so much in the news in the run-up to its introduction, with the British Medical Association holding out against it to the last minute and headline stories predicting a limitless demand for free corsets and wigs. And then the day came, and instead of hearing about the panel I started hearing about capitation fees, and Aneurin Bevan was on the cover of *Time* magazine, and there wasn't a crisis about corsets and wigs after all – though I was glad NHS doctors were allowed to prescribe stout where they thought it appropriate, because it meant that Guinness would keep sending us their witty coloured booklets (collectors' items today), with illustrations by Rex Whistler and others.

As for antibiotics and the other 'wonder drugs' which came in during the post-war years, we have learned that they have their drawbacks, and that they can't cure everything; above all, we have learned to take them for granted. In an age which prefers not to count its blessings, the very term 'wonder drug' is an embarrass-ment. But if getting rid of diphtheria and beating back tuberculosis aren't wonderful, what is? Only a fool could look back at the twentieth century and retain a simple faith in the religion of Progress; but you would have to be hard-hearted, or dishonest, to have lived through the medical revolution of the middle years of the century and pretend that progress never happened.

At the same time it is irritating to come across younger doctors – I have met one or two – who talk as though real medicine only began in 1945. Certainly practitioners of an earlier generation recognised how limited their resources were, and how ineffective most of their remedies. Writing in the 1930s, Harry Roberts, the best-known East End GP of the day, quoted with amusement and a fair degree of approval the cynical maxim that 'the best physician is the one who knows the worthlessness of the most drugs'. But that doesn't mean that Roberts didn't also feel that there had been a good deal of progress in the thirty years since he had arrived in the East End. Everything is relative: the little that had been accomplished in those years seemed quite a lot at the time. And though much of the improvement had been the result of better living conditions, drugs had played a certain part. My father had shared in the general enthusiasm when M & B was introduced in the thirties – here at last was a drug that could do something for pneumonia – and as a diabetic he took a special interest in insulin. Banting and Best, the Canadians who had first made it available for medical purposes in the 1920s, were honoured names.

Where a doctor couldn't effect a cure, he could at least offer hope or reassurance; he could try to alleviate symptoms (which to a patient in pain is a lot better than nothing), or to create the best conditions for nature to work its own cure (which it often did). Long before human beings could cure anything, except by accident, they established the principle of healing: it was the first step.

I was curious, as I grew up, about the profession – about what doctors were like, rather than what they did. The *British Medical Journal* used to arrive in the post on Fridays, rolled up like a scroll. When I dipped into it, what interested me most were the obituaries, and the gossipy notes which used to appear under the heading 'Nova et Vetera'. (It sounded so much better in Latin.) I cherished stories, many of them no doubt apocryphal, about old physicians and surgeons: a favourite was the one about the surgeon who was supposed to have remarked, in the course of an operation, 'Mr Anaesthetist, if the patient can keep awake, surely you can.' And needless to say there were the scandals. Some, such as the tricks used by rogue GPs to poach patients from their colleagues, were relatively humdrum. A few were more sensational. The big local affair of my childhood was the case of the GP who was sent to jail after a girl died during an illegal abortion. I sometimes thought of him, and wondered what had become of him. He had been struck off, of course; it occurs to me now that after he got out he probably specialised almost exclusively in abortions. At a time when the alternative was often the legendary old woman with a knitting needle, there was a place for him.

Gloomy concerns like these were a world away from the spacious calm of Harley Street. My father had a number of patients who could afford private consultations with a specialist. He would accompany them, and whenever possible turn the occasion into a family outing, parking us in a tea shop nearby. London W1 made a pleasant change from London E3. Once or twice I was taken to see a specialist myself; we had a Harley Street dentist, too; and there was a memorable consultation, when I was nine, with a surgeon called Sir James Walton. He was a Scotsman, who did his best to put me at my ease (he insisted on addressing me as 'laddie'), but who could hardly fail to strike awe: he was going to cut me open, and he was the first 'Sir' I had ever met. But then I was deeply impressed – the more so because I really knew so little of it – by Harley Street as a whole. Everything there seemed so polished and burnished and commodious. Later on, when I read Henry James, I realised that I was mentally furnishing his drawing rooms with details gleaned from glimpses of Harley Street interiors.

Later on, I also learned to be a bit more sceptical. It became clear that the great men of the profession – Belloc's 'physicians of the utmost fame' – were not always as great as they were painted. Doctors themselves, although they had to be careful what they said in public, often turned out when they spoke in private to have a less than enchanted view of eminent colleagues, and of the arts by which they had risen. You heard how this one excelled at indirect self-promotion, how that one had ruthlessly cultivated a chance royal connection. Literature, too, sowed its doubts. Perhaps the satire of Molière in *L'Amour médecin* and *Le Malade imaginaire* was out of date. Perhaps. But there were always the consultants in *The Doctor's Dilemma*, with their pet nostrums – my father could quote the jokes about stimulating the phagocytes and cutting out the nuciform sac – and their bland professional solidarity. They were only caricatures, of course, but caricatures with a point.

I still found, in spite of all the question marks, that the idea of Harley Street appealed to my imagination. I wanted my consultants to look distinguished and wise, just as I wanted my leading QCs to be larger than life, and my bishops to be ripe Trollopean dignitaries. And if that sounds frivolous, or unduly literary, there were better grounds for being impressed as well. Most consultants, as far as I could judge, got results where the means were available, and the best of them were remarkable men. Geoffrey Keynes, for instance. In our house the name Keynes generally signified Geoffrey rather than his brother Maynard, and Geoffrey Keynes the surgeon rather than the Geoffrey Keynes who (wearing his other hat, as they say) was the editor of Blake and the bibliographer of Donne. He had joined the surgical team at Bart's after serving in the First World War; in the course of a career which combined medical practice and literary scholarship in almost equal measure, he had carried out pioneer work on blood transfusion, written the life of William Harvey, compiled some twenty learned bibliographies, and found time in the midst of it all to devise a ballet based on the Book of Job for Vaughan Williams. He lived on into his nineties, and I was delighted to hear from a bibliographer friend who had mentioned my name to him some time in the 1970s (apropos of the *Times Literary Supplement*, which I was then editing) that he remembered my father and spoke well of him.

Of all the big Harley Street names, the one I heard invoked most often was that of Lord Horder. He had been my father's teacher at Bart's, and my father's admiration for him never wavered. It was inspired, in the first instance, by his fabled skill as a diagnostician, his ability to spot clues and make connections. My father, if the tributes of patients or colleagues are to be believed, was an unusually skilled diagnostician himself. But whenever he received a compliment to that effect, he would say to my mother afterwards, 'I owe it all to Horder.' He used to call him 'the greatest detective in London'.

A flair for diagnosis can, I suppose, exist in a kind of moral vacuum, as a purely technical skill. There is a striking passage in Proust, where Marcel's parents consult Dr Cottard, and this hitherto despised member of the Verdurins' little clan, socially 'an imbecile', proves at one rapid stroke to be a physician of genius. In Horder's case, however, clinical genius was plainly inseparable from an ability to understand and assess human beings. My father admired this aspect of his teaching almost as much as its more strictly scientific content. One remark which he never forgot was, 'You are going to be doctors, and however much anatomy or physiology you have to study this year, you should try to find time to read a few novels.' Patients were people as well as organisms.

All the characteristics of Horder which I heard about are confirmed and enlarged on in the biography by his son Mervyn Horder. When I read it, I was particularly stirred by the fact that in the course of the speech he gave when he retired from Bart's, he spoke of 'Shakespeare and Molière and Cervantes and the other great clinical observers'.

I never asked my father whether he regretted not having gone on to become a specialist himself. In practice, the prospect had not arisen, as it probably hadn't for most of the other Jewish doctors of his generation who worked in the East End. Some of them might well have ended up in prominent positions if they had started out under more favourable circumstances; as it is, they stayed on to become valued members of the community. Focal members, too, since they were expected to dispense guidance and advice as well as medicine. They didn't quite form a group – they were too busy, too locked into their own practices, to see much of one another – but in terms of the background they shared and the common conditions under which they worked, they perhaps constituted a type. Their names were familiar to me from early on. Steinberg, Sacks (the father of Oliver Sacks), Frohlich, Caplan . . . Hard-working men, though if there had been a vote for the outstanding personality among them, it would in all likelihood have gone to a woman – Hannah Billig, a legend far beyond Cable Street, where she had her practice, and a recipient of the George Medal for bravery during an air raid. (She continued visiting shelters to tend the injured, even though she had a broken ankle.) I never met her, but I was lucky enough to become friendly with another fine doctor, Maurice Marcus. He was a man of broad sympathies, with a strong interest in the arts. One of his patients was the writer Colin MacInnes, who lived for a time in Spitalfields. Subsequently, when MacInnes lay dying in a hospital in Kent, he used to visit him and smuggle in drugs which the hospital had forbidden, in order to ease the pain of his last few weeks.

Relations between the Jewish doctors of East London and their non-Jewish colleagues were, as far as I know, good. The point is worth stressing, because there is another, less agreeable story to be told about British medicine in the 1930s. From the moment Hitler came to power, the leading British medical organisations campaigned against the admission or employment of Jewish refugee doctors on all but the most limited scale. Lord Dawson of Penn, President of the Royal College of Physicians, set the tone in a memorandum to the Home Office in 1933, in which he maintained that 'the number of foreign doctors who could teach us anything could be counted on the fingers of one hand'. (This at a time when German medicine – in which Jews had played a conspicuous part – led the world.) Nor was the role of professional bodies confined to mere lobbying. They also helped to formulate and apply a whole series of restrictive policies; and although their immediate motives seem to have been protectionist rather than anti-Semitic, it isn't always easy to tell where one set of objections ended and the other began.

How does one reconcile this sorry episode with my impression of good relations in the East End? Several possible explanations come to mind: differences between attitudes to refugees and attitudes to doctors who had grown up here; regional variations; differences between the elite of the profession and ordinary GPs. And I could simply be wrong.

Where I can speak with confidence is in respect of a few cases which I observed at first hand – above all in respect of my father's closest colleague, Dr Craig. Stanley Paul Craig practised in Burdett Road (the road where there had been a famous political fracas in the 1880s which had led to the arrest of William Morris). He and my father used to cover for each other during holidays and emergencies, an arrangement which continued for many years in perfect amity. He was a Scotsman, very much so, with a broad episcopal brow; when we visited him the whisky was immediately produced, and my parents – no great drinkers – were invited to 'raise their elbows'. The Craig–Gross friendship even survived an embarrassing episode during one visit (I must have been eleven or twelve at the time) when my father proudly produced a poem I had written and got me to read it. Dr Craig listened politely, made a kind comment and reached for the whisky again.

There were other examples of cordial relations with colleagues – with Gordon Sears, for instance, a physician at the local Mile End hospital, who took particular pleasure in talking about his daughter Heather, a girl of my age who wanted to be an actress. (She went on to star in the film of *Room at the Top*.) But a more significant gauge of how little racial disharmony cast a shadow over my father's work was his relationship with his patients.

About half of them, at a guess, were Jewish, though the proportion dropped as Jews continued to leave the district. He inevitably had a more intimate understanding of some of their personal problems than a non-Jewish doctor would have had; he could also speak to them, if the need arose, in Yiddish. But it wasn't all smooth sailing. He had a handful of impossibly demanding patients, and in private he used to complain that most of them were Jewish. Sometimes he sounded utterly fed up with them, but he tried to make a joke of the problem where he could, and he laughed when he heard that another Jewish doctor had coined a term for the condition from which some of *his* Jewish patients were suffering – 'GMG', which stood for *goornisht mit goornisht*, which means 'nothing with nothing'.

Most of his non-Jewish patients, in the more homogeneous London of those days, were English or Irish. His popularity with them was attested in countless ways. Many of them, for instance, were members of the local Catholic church, the Guardian Angels, and when he suffered his first coronary thrombosis, an official of the church – the sacristan, I think – came running round almost at once to tell my mother how upset they had all been by the news that 'our doctor' was ill. In the later years of his life, in the fifties, West Indian families began to move into the district, and he got on very well with them, too. He was tickled that at last he had patients who didn't address him as 'Doctor'. They called him 'Doc' instead.

Looking back, I realise the extent to which medicine provided him with a bridge to the non-Jewish world. It was also, for someone starting out where he did, the classic career open to talents. Every Jew worth his salt knows a few jokes about 'my son the doctor'. But it would be hopelessly narrow to think of medicine primarily in terms of social advancement or (in cases like his) acculturation. The career, once taken up, becomes – to a greater or lesser degree – an end in itself. For all but the most selfish, it entails a genuine ideal of service.

One of my friends, Max Rayne, is a multimillionaire (and a great philanthropist) who began life in the humblest circumstances. Between the wars he and his family were patients of my father, and one incident, around the time of George V's Silver Jubilee, fixed my father's character in his mind for ever. There was fever in the house; there was also very little money – everyone was out of a job. My father, who had been summoned, conducted his examination. His normal fee for a visit would have been sixpence, but when the time came to pay he told them to forget it.

I was touched by the story, but I recount it here because I am convinced that in similar circumstances thousands of other doctors would have done the same. Dr Johnson, in his life of the physician-poet Samuel Garth in the *Lives of the Poets*, praised physicians for their 'liberality and dignity of sentiment', and their 'willingness to exert a lucrative art, where there is no hope of lucre'. He was writing in his most encomiastic mode: not every doctor deserves such a tribute. But I believe that enough good ones do for it to be an essential part of the picture.

5

A Small Town in Surrey

EGHAM: A characterless village on the Thames . . . keeping
a winding main street without any worthwhile buildings in it.

– Ian Nairn and Nikolaus Pevsner, *The Buildings
of England: Surrey*

My story began in the East End. The 'natural' progression, the
standard path followed by the children of immigrants, ought to
have been from the East End outwards, never to return. But first
the war intervened, and we left London. Then, some seven years
later, the circumstances of my father's work meant that we were
back where we had started. I began in the East End, and no doubt
the geography of my earliest years stamped me in ways I am not
aware of; but for practical purposes, I was a product of the Home
Counties before I became an East Ender.

When the war started my father was determined to get us out of
London as soon as he could. Nobody knew quite what to expect,
but Stanley Baldwin's warning that 'the bomber will always get
through' still reverberated; doctors had been told to prepare to
deal with heavy casualties and Mile End was in the danger zone,
close to the docks. So in the autumn of 1939 we were whisked off
to a farm in Shropshire – 'we' being my mother, my brother (who
was only a couple of months old) and myself.

Where exactly in Shropshire the farm was I don't know. Nor do
I know how long we stayed there; possibly it was for as little as
two or three weeks. But the experience made a deep impression. In

one respect I had been prepared for it: hopeless townie though I was, my favourite toy back in London had been a rudimentary toy farm, presided over by a little wooden figure called Farmer Giles. I had spent happy hours simply pushing little wooden cows and sheep around the carpet. But this was the real thing.

Of the memories which remain today, the clearest, apart from one of poking around in a hedge, are the smells – the smells (by no means disagreeable) of the stable and cowshed; delicious smells in the kitchen, where the farmer's wife, a tall woman in a long white apron, used to bake her own bread. And beyond that, there was a general sense of friendliness, of being made welcome. I can't recall anything frightening or forbidding.

There is a poem by Gerard Manley Hopkins called 'In the Valley of the Elwy' which moves me to the point of tears, the opening lines in particular:

> I remember a house where all were good
> To me, God knows, deserving no such thing . . .

The Elwy is a river in North Wales, and it occurred to me one day that what lay behind my response, or at any rate deepened it, was a buried memory of my time in Shropshire, so close to the Welsh border. Perhaps that is far-fetched; but I know that Shropshire was important to me. My first real experience of life away from home, it must have helped to lay down a substratum of trust, an expectation that the world would prove friendly rather than not.

There is another consideration, although I can't have been conscious of it at the time. The farm was the first non-Jewish home I had ever stayed in, and we were almost certainly the first Jews whom the farmer's family had ever met, but there doesn't seem to have been any strain or hostility on that account. Or was I merely unaware of what was going on? Some years ago, reading an interview with the politician Julian Critchley, I found myself confronted by his description of his mother as 'bitterly anti-Semitic in a kind of Shropshire-working-class way'. It certainly gave me a jolt; but it wasn't enough to destroy my childhood image of Shropshire, or to persuade me that I had been deluded about the goodwill with which we had been received.

One episode reinforces that feeling. There was a boy on the farm called Joe: he was probably about twelve, though he seemed older. On the day we were leaving he offered me one of his treasures, a small pile of copies of the *Beano* and *Dandy*. I said no, because I wasn't able to read well enough yet to make anything of them. A year or two later, I recalled my refusal with chagrin – all the more so because they had been pre-war issues, looking very thick and colourful in comparison with their skimpy wartime successors. But I also recalled his kindness.

From Shropshire we moved to Sussex – to Bracklesham Bay, a mere speck on the map, a few miles south of Chichester. It was here that I first went to school, in a village hall where we listened to a programme called *Music and Movement* on the BBC, and did all the things that five-year-olds were supposed to. My chief memory, however, is of my first visit to the cinema, and its consequences. Children of my generation tended to be traumatised by either the witch in *Snow White* or the witch in *The Wizard of Oz*. In my case it was *The Wizard of Oz*, which I was taken to see in Chichester. For weeks afterwards, I was haunted by the idea of witches. In particular, I became convinced that a witch was lurking behind the tall hedge in front of a house which we passed on the way to and from school. And my anxieties were soon overlaid by fresh ones. I was either trying to read or being read to from a book which contained a jokey episode, complete with comic-strip illustrations, about cannibals. I asked my mother what they were and when she wouldn't tell me, I began brooding. I wondered whether they weren't out there in the dark, along with the witches. (I pictured them as small, goblin-like creatures, which is how they had been portrayed in the book.) I became afraid of going to the bathroom at night, in case they were lying in wait for me in the passage.

Fortunately, these fears soon subsided, and never returned to plague me again. They were the kind of fantasies which could have assailed a small child at any time – but had I also been infected by the adult anxieties which were in the air? It seems highly unlikely, but I suppose it is just possible. For it was a period of great apprehension, the period of the fall of France. The south coast suddenly looked dangerously exposed; I am not sure we would have been allowed to go on living there. But the question didn't arise, since we were already planning to move. My father had bought a house in Egham, and we arrived there a few days after Dunkirk.

When I look back at the town where I was to spend the greater part of my childhood, I think of it first of all in terms neither of characters nor incidents, but topography. It wasn't a very big town, but it was big enough to explore, and go on exploring, big enough to retain unknown areas even after I had been there for years.* It seemed to have grown naturally, too: it had an irregular layout, with all kinds of loops and byways and unexpected transitions.

We lived in an unfinished street consisting of a dozen or so brand-new houses, the beginning of a development which had been abandoned at the outbreak of war. On one side lay fields. On the other side, leading back to the main parts of town, three roads fanned out – all of them Victorian or Edwardian, which made us seem all the more modern in comparison. To the left, Limes Avenue was leafy enough to live up to its name – a street of villas, interrupted near the other end by one of the town's many reminders of a recent rural past, a smithy. (Even when the smith wasn't working – and he was admirably, classically brawny – it was satisfying just to take a peek at the anvil.) To the right, North Street led on to a region of proletarian terraces and a footbridge over the railway known as 'Jacob's Ladder'. In between, Grange Road was the route to the centre of town. It seemed to go on and on and on, but the journey along it was punctuated by landmarks: the house to be hurried past, where a boy had fallen to his death from a garden wall; the house where the 'old cat woman' lived surrounded by her pets like so many familiars (but I had lost my fear of witches); the house with pampas grass in front of it; the house with the laburnum tree. I knew, when I revisited it as an adult, that it was going to be a much shorter road than I had recalled, but I still wasn't prepared for it to be quite as short as it was.

* Why Nairn and Pevsner in the quotation at the head of this chapter should describe it as 'a village' is a mystery.

At first I was naturally only allowed out for walks with an adult. (For a time, my chief joy, to the irritation of anyone accompanying me, was to trail a stick across railings or the overlapping slats of fences.) Quite early on, though, I began to go out by myself: the streets were safe, the wartime traffic was light. It became an adventure simply to try and work out how one bit of the town related to another – to discover that if you went down the turning off Station Road which you had never taken before, it led to a lane which led to a path which led to an alley which came out in the high street, and which you had thought up till then was a dead end. I was intrigued by the cut-through between two nearby residential streets – a dark featureless passageway, except that in the middle you suddenly came across a workshop full of saddles and horse brasses. I was thrilled to learn that there was a 'secret' route from the high street to the street where we lived, if you circled round through Sweeps Lane, a muddy track with cottages on one side (the gardens always seemed to be full of squalling children) and open land with blackberry bushes on the other. A few of the streets I explored were picturesque, most were completely commonplace. But 'commonplace' isn't a word children know.

As the mysteries of interconnection were slowly mastered, a new fascination succeeded: the long straggling high street. Here the pleasure was one of knowledge attained – of familiarity with the precise manner in which the street narrowed and broadened, with the subtle changes of character from one stretch to another, with the exact order of the shops. And the shops themselves were varied enough and seductive enough to prevent my enjoyment from growing stale. It is odd. On occasional trips to London, when my mother took me round the big West End stores, I was utterly bored. ('Peter Robinson' and 'D.H. Evans' became names synonymous with tedium.) But I never tired of some of the shops in Egham – the hairdresser's, with a green, vaguely oriental statuette squatting in the window, advertising Eugene permanent waves; the greengrocer's with a cardboard cut-out of bananas dangling from the ceiling, courtesy of Fyffe's (especially enticing, because bananas were unobtainable 'for the duration', and I couldn't remember what they tasted like); the baker's, where amiable full-breasted Mrs Burgess, a Frenchwoman who had married an English soldier during the First World War, spoke perfect English but added up your bill in French.

True, there was one early trauma. As a very small boy I was encouraged go into a shop by myself (possibly for the first time) to buy some small item: it was all part of learning to be more independent. The shopkeeper, a bald man with bulging eyes, was standing behind the counter. As soon as I entered he barked at me – very ferociously, as it seemed – and I raced out again, my heart in my mouth. It was one of the most frightening moments of my childhood. But it can't have put me off shops for long. I soon took as much interest in what went on inside them as in their window displays – in the roller dispensing brown wrapping paper; in the brass weights lined up like giant chess pieces; in the man who cut cheese with a wire.

It probably helped, made everything seem more distinctive, that most of them were small and family-owned. The only big chains I remember in the town were the now long-defunct grocery stores the Home and Colonial (*there*'s a name from another era) and David Greig. But in other respects mass-marketing had of course already remade the world. Its products lay all around us, and very beguiling they were – though in most cases it wasn't so much the possibility of acquiring them that appealed to me as the way they were presented. I loved packaging, trade marks, slogans, placards, catalogues, the lettering of brand names, the pictures on boxes and tins. The more exotic-sounding names, at least, had a positive ring of poetry about them: Mazawattee, Triang, Kia-Ora ('pronounced Kee-Ora'), O-Cedar, Sylvan flakes. I was captivated by the wit of 'Did you Maclean your teeth today?', and transfixed by the confident announcement that 'Britons make it, it makes Britons' (that was Shredded Wheat). And a whole raft of characters seemed to inhabit their own fairy-tale universe: Bertie Bassett, the man about town constructed entirely of liquorice allsorts; Mr Therm, advertising gas; the Quaker on the box of Quaker Oats; the anthropomorphised orange and lemon advertising Idris ('when I's dry'); the fat man searching for the tin of Andrews' Salts which was all the time in his hip pocket ('I must have left it behind').

Only two other buildings along the high street rivalled the shops for interest. One, indeed, eventually surpassed them – the Savoy Cinema, the town's dream-palace (small though it was) and in due course my own. The other was the public library. I was too young to use it, but I was drawn to the panel outside displaying the dust jackets – garish affairs, usually – of recent acquisitions. Dornford Yates and the Whiteoaks saga of Mazo de la Roche seemed particularly well represented; so was the not very distinguished crime writer Sidney Horler, creator of a virile hero called Tiger Standish. I also used to linger over the noticeboard alongside announcing the productions of the local theatrical group, the Madcaps. Another puzzle: what exactly was a madcap?

All these urban pleasures were ten minutes' walk away, but it took only thirty seconds to find yourself out in the country. Leave the house by the garden gate, and there were a couple of houses on the left, then an interesting scrap of unclaimed ground, then a ditch and an untidy hedge, and beyond that fields stretching to the horizon – farmland, though there didn't seem to be any problem about roaming around it.

> Harum-scarum childhood plays
> In the meadows near his home . . .

I was never a particularly harum-scarum child, still less a particularly daring one; but it was impossible not to feel liberated in the fields, not to play Cowboys and Indians or climb trees (if only to the lower branches) or go searching for new sources of conkers. The surrounding life had its charms, too. The cows were amiable; there was a thrill, for a town child, in stumbling across a simple rabbit hole. But not everything was idyllic. The farmer himself gave me pause: he looked the part, in his battered old hat, but he had a mean face, and I was once shocked to see how viciously he hit a cow on the flank with his switch as he drove it along. It wasn't at all how I'd imagined Farmer Giles.

There was also an unpleasant episode which, no doubt quite unfairly, was to remain for ever associated in my mind with rural life. I had been playing in the fields with a boy connected with the farm, whom I didn't really know: we must both have been eight or nine. When we had run around enough, we sat on the grass and he proceeded to give me the first sex instruction I had ever had, apart from some vague remarks from my parents about where I had come from. His chosen theme was menstruation, which he described in graphic colloquial detail, with talk about 'jam-rags' and the like. Naturally I was interested; but there was no mistaking his aggresive tone, or his triumphant sense that now we both knew something degrading about girls.

Across the street from our house there was an acre or so of rising ground, fenced in but unkempt, with the stump of a large tree about halfway up which made an excellent platform for standing on and proclaiming oneself king of the castle. (The tree had been sawn down not long before – as part of the interrupted scheme, I imagine, for building houses.) At the top of this field stood a cottage with a cluttered, tobacco-ey interior. The family who lived in it were country people; they asked me in for tea once or twice and were always friendly, though on one occasion – it was the day of a big race – they couldn't help laughing out loud when I revealed that I didn't know what a bookmaker was. Behind the cottage there were close-standing trees, and paths leading to Egham Hill; and when you came out on the hill you could get glimpses of something truly romantic and mysterious – the turreted chateau of Royal Holloway College, modelled on Chambord, looking like a setting for *Beauty and the Beast*.

At this point you left the town behind you and entered new regions, which we visited seldom enough for them to retain a mythic quality. Englefield Green will always conjure up the memory of the end of a summer afternoon under a broad golden sky; Virginia Water means above all an excited exploration among silver birch trees and bracken. A little further off lay the smooth, purring prosperity of Ascot and Sunningdale, while the closeness of Windsor conferred an ultimate prestige on the area. My own principal memory of 'the proud Keep of Windsor' is ignominious, however. On some kind of outing, a couple of other boys and I cheeked one of the castle sentries. By the time we got home I had started worrying, and for days afterwards I half-expected the police or even royal messengers to show up with a summons.

Daily life in Egham itself held few such adventures. You kept seeing the same characters on the streets, although I can only recall one or two of the more distinctive-looking ones – the brisk little man who went phut-phutting along on a motor scooter; the big man with pink mask-like features who had been horribly muti-lated (I assumed in the First World War) and patched together by some primitive plastic surgery. I was also impressed, chiefly because they made me feel uncomfortable, by the Shepherds, the family with whom my maternal grandmother lodged, a couple of streets away. (She had originally come to stay with us, but there had been tensions, and she had moved out.) The Shepherds were from Lancashire, the first Northerners I had ever met, and perhaps it was just a natural abrasiveness of manner which made me feel that they were perpetually on the point of coming to blows. Their son Billy was at any rate prepared to pass the time with me, even though he was several years older. He was adept at making model aeroplanes, and tried to introduce me, without success, to the pleasures of balsa wood and glue.

Socially our street, Spring Avenue, formed a fairly self-contained enclave. Three other boys of my own age lived there. Two of them were inseparable friends. They were both of Irish descent, their fathers were both teachers and they both went to the same Catholic school. My relations with them were cool, without being actively hostile. The third boy, Bruce, was much more friendly, though a bit boring. His father, who was a photographer on a tabloid paper, once called a residents' meeting and made the alarming proposal (fortunately nothing came of it) that the children in the street should be subjected to extra doses of sport, since we weren't getting enough exercise. In other respects, however, he seemed a decent enough type. His wife, Bruce's mother, was an ardent amateur soprano. Her performances provoked a good deal of embarrassment (if you were her children) or mirth (if you were their friends).

The neighbour my mother saw the most of, Mrs Marcey, was the only career woman living on Spring Avenue (she worked on the Stock Exchange), and the nearest thing to a scarlet woman that the street had to offer, too. She originally came from Dublin, and another lesson in life's complexities was being made to realise that not everyone who came from that city was a Catholic. Mrs Marcey, though I doubt whether religion played any great part in her life, was a Protestant; her mother was furiously anti-Catholic, and used to say she had never been happy living in Ireland on account of 'the black beetles' (meaning nuns and priests). Mrs Marcey's husband Fred, on the other hand, was far removed from such acrimony. He was a cheerful, stocky, crinkly-eyed Home Counties type, who looked more at home in a blazer than a suit. Given the chance, he would probably have been happy to while away the rest of his life at the cricket club or in the pub. But Mrs Marcey was energetic and ambitious, and had carved out a position for herself in a stockbroker's office at a time when there can have been very few other women in the field. She had also become the girlfriend of a rather shady Jewish businessman – let's call him Landau. (When he met my father in Egham, he tried to get him to act as a nominee in a share-buying scheme; when my father declined, he turned up at the surgery and tried to bully him into changing his mind.)

The Marceys' marriage was coming apart, amid dramas of which I sometimes caught a glimpse. There was the time when Mrs Marcey took me to see a film at the Savoy. When we got back, there was a great flap: the electric fire in her drawing room was on, and she was *fairly* sure she had switched it off; a cushion was lying dangerously near it. Did she really suspect dear old Fred (who at that stage had left home) of breaking in and planning a little blaze? On another occasion, I had dropped by to deliver a message one morning when the great Landau appeared from the bedroom, where he had obviously spent the night – a bulky, grey-haired figure in an expensive maroon dressing gown. He was surly and peremptory, but I still found something glamorous in the half-understood situation.

I owe another stage in my sexual education to the Marceys – indirectly, at least. They had a nephew, a boy of my own age who sometimes stayed with them. One day they took us both up to London to see the Tower, and while we were going round he told me he had found out that there was something very important called 'doing' – that men 'did' women and quite possibly women 'did' men. He wouldn't or couldn't elaborate, and it was all very confusing; but at least it helped to explain why Mrs Mopp, the charwoman on the radio series ITMA, was always greeted with a gale of laughter from the audience when she asked the boss, 'Can I do you now, sir?'

In the sedate world of Spring Avenue, the Marceys represented a splash of colour. Virtually all our other neighbours 'fitted in', the only exceptions being a young couple called Campion. There wasn't much colour there: they were mild unassuming people, whose lives largely revolved around a rather snively small daughter. What set them apart was that they were tarred with the brush of being working class. Not literally working class: they could hardly have afforded to live in the Avenue on a workman's wage, and Mr Campion was in fact some kind of technician. But they were working class in origin, working class – however faintly – in accent and manner. It was all fairly oblique. No one was positively unfriendly to them; no one ignored them. But there was a coolness, even so. Constant small signs made it clear that they weren't quite the equals of anyone else in the street.

This was a lesson in the nuances of class. Broader class-distinctions had of course been apparent from the first, and my sense of them was reinforced by some of my early experiences at school. When we arrived in Egham I was enrolled in the nearest junior school – a council school, probably a good deal less rough than such an establishment would have been in London, but still (or so I imagine) preponderantly working class. I can't have been particularly unhappy there, since I remember almost nothing about it, and those few memories I do have are mostly benign. But I don't think I learned much, and I know that my mother began worrying about the strange things that were happening to my accent. I can recall her correcting me when I said 'it's my-un', just like the other children, instead of 'it's mine'.

When I left, it was to be sent to a private school run by a Mrs Brown, whose bourgeois credentials were not in doubt – one of those schools which by a curious arrangement took girls up to the age of seventeen or eighteen and a small number of boys up to the age of eight or nine. The teaching there was more thorough than anything I had known up till then, but it was mostly dull. We had writing books with sentences printed in copperplate at the top of each page ('Sumatra is a source of camphor', 'Plumbago is a product of Ceylon'), which we had to copy out five or six times underneath. We were expected to know exactly how many yards there were in a rod, pole or perch. It was disagreeable, too, that when we misbehaved we were rapped on the knuckles with a ruler; and we seem to have spent an inordinate amount of time making things out of raffia. But there were compensations. I enjoyed the songs we were taught, for instance: I remember one sunny morning when I felt unaccountably happy just because we were singing 'Dashing Away with the Smoothing-Iron'. And the presence of all those girls must have stirred me in more ways than I was aware.

As it is, two memories stand out. One is no more than a snapshot: a pageant with the head girl up on the stage playing Britannia, complete with property-box helmet, trident and shield, and with a thrillingly off-the-shoulder robe. The second memory is more extended: I became attached to a girl in my own class called Barbara, known to her family as 'Barbary', and I was invited home to have lunch with her – a journey into unfamiliar territory, since she lived near Chertsey, four or five miles away. She had red hair, and wore a red gingham dress, and at lunch her mother served a strawberry junket: everything blended together into a general sense of delicious pinkness. Alas, I left the school soon afterwards and never saw her again. It wasn't until two or three years later that I found myself smitten to the same degree – by Madeleine Carroll, whom I saw in *The Prisoner of Zenda* at the Savoy.

At the age of nine I started out at my next school – boys only – and the reign of Mrs Brown gave way to the altogether more memorable reign of Mrs Gittins. Violet Gittins ran her school from home. Her husband, Captain Gittins, had served in India, and on the odd occasions when you were allowed into the private part of the house almost the first objects you saw were some brass pots and pans which she identified as 'Benares ware'. There were just two classes in the school; she took the senior one herself, and left the junior one to an assistant called Mrs Chater, who was very much under her thumb. But then she had the general air of someone who expected to be obeyed. She was a strict disciplinarian, who used the cane (though I was spared her attentions in that respect), and she took it for granted that her writ ran beyond the school itself: I was once reported to her by dutiful Mrs Chater, who had spotted me on the street riding a bike with only one hand. Behind her back she was known by the boys, just to show we weren't going to be overwhelmed by her, as 'Old Ma Gits'.

Yet within her limits, she was a good teacher – clear and methodical; a demon for spelling and grammar, as you might expect, but also adept at bringing to life history, geography and especially poetry. She could hold the class, or anyone in it who was capable of being held, with her renditions and explanations of *John Gilpin* and *Barbara Frietchie* ('Shoot, if you must, this old grey head . . .') and Goldsmith's poem about the man bitten by a mad dog. Another speciality, approached in a more competitive spirit than most modern educationalists would approve of, was 'mental arithmetic'. I usually got the correct answer in first, until the day when a newcomer joined the class, a tall skinny boy called Martin Dodsworth who quickly established that he was faster than I was. (He has since become a well-known professor of English, and the editor, together with my old Oxford tutor John Bamborough, of the works of Robert Burton.)

What was finally being taught was 'a certain idea of England' – *Hymns Ancient and Modern* (we sang one every morning), fair play, the King's English, the Mother of Parliaments, trial by jury, Hearts of Oak, the bulldog breed, the Lady with the Lamp, the Workshop of the World, the RSPCA, Magna Carta ('What say the reeds at Runnymede?' – and we were reminded that Runnymede was on the river only a mile or two away). It was understood without much difficulty that for essential purposes England also meant Britain; and the Empire, including India, was still firmly in the background, not so much a political institution (or so it seemed to a nine-year-old) as a large fact of nature. Within two or three years even Mrs Gittins would have been unable to inculcate the same imperial picture. But in 1944 Midnight's Children had not yet been born, and it was still just possible for English children to grow up believing that India was 'ours'. My own sense of the Anglo-Indian connection was heightened by the fact that I was going through my cigarette-card phase, and the set I was keenest to collect was Wills' gorgeously coloured 'Indian Regiments'.

In isolating the element of patriotism in the schooling we received, I am in danger of making it sound more programmatic than it was. We were seldom subjected to outright pep talks; the message was mostly conveyed through incidental details or asides. No 'patriotic' moment sticks more clearly in my mind than one which occurred during a lesson about South America, when we were told in passing that South American traders used to seal their bargains 'on the word of an Englishman'. That was all that was said on the subject – and it was enough.

It wasn't only at school that Englishness was instilled. The whole town offered a daily lesson in the subject, simply by being what it was. And meanwhile my Jewish life at this period, as I have said, was largely confined to home.

The sense of contrast between the two worlds, English and Jewish, ran deep. I must sometimes have felt, even then, as though I had been assigned simultaneous roles in two different plays. Yet I can't recall being especially troubled by this dual destiny. What it principally suggested was not so much conflict as inconsistency.

This is partly, no doubt, because I hardly ever thought about it. Like most children, I took things as they came. Nor was I faced with a stark opposition between family and outside world. Even at home, the life we led was largely 'English', and not very different in most respects from that of our neighbours.

Still, the crucial factor has to be that I never suffered on account of being Jewish, never felt that my future was hemmed in, never endured either literal or metaphorical blows. The general attitude I encountered was one of casual acceptance. When I did well at school, I received encouragement from teachers. In the playground, even the boys who disliked me never flung the fact that I was Jewish in my face. And though there were occasional minor embarrassments, they were just that, embarrassments. The worst one I can remember was far from being evidence of ill will. I had been invited to spend the day with a boy called Duncan; his mother, anxious not to offend Jewish dietary scruples, had taken care to avoid serving meat for lunch, but inadvertently served crab salad instead. I felt bad about not eating it (I pretended that I just didn't like it), and worse when Duncan's mother (who must have guessed the real reason) did her best to put me at my ease and went straight out to the kitchen to whip up something else.

I have heard and read very different accounts by Jewish contemporaries, of English childhoods in which anti-Semitism cast a serious shadow. I have also read accounts by historians detailing the widespread extent of anti-Semitism in wartime England (and even its actual growth). So am I deluding myself about my own childhood? I can only say that I have racked my brains and searched my memories, and that I don't think so. And if I am right, how do I explain my good fortune? It undoubtedly improved my chances that I wasn't an evacuee, that I wasn't quartered on another family or dependent on strangers. Beyond that, I have no better explanation than luck. A single malignant neighbour or teacher or schoolfellow would have made all the difference. So I can only speak for myself – although at the same time I can't help wondering whether recent historians have sometimes made out the situation to be worse than it was. Not by exaggerating the presence of prejudice, but by giving insufficient weight to its extensive absence. The history of non-anti-Semitism remains an unwritten subject.

I have been talking purely about my own experience, of how I was treated and spoken to myself. What I overheard or sensed may well have been more significant. Even here, there is nothing outstandingly awful to report. Some of the anti-Semitic vibes I was to pick up in later life – as an undergraduate in civilised Oxford, for instance – were uglier than anything I ever heard in Egham. But that prejudice was lurking out there was never in doubt, and even as a small child one learned to be on the alert for the scratch of its claws.

I can't recall the context in which I overheard a woman teacher at the council school speaking in bitter tones about *them*, for instance; but young as I was, I understood at once who she meant. A subsequent incident came closer home. The only Jewish-owned shop in the town, as far as I know, was a small establishment in the high street, the Bargain Box, which sold knitting wool and minor items of haberdashery. It was run by a woman called Hetty Slenoff, a temporary exile from London. My grandmother spent a good deal of time there, nattering about this and that, and one day, when I heard someone refer to it as 'the Jew shop', I felt as though she were being personally targeted.

Then, later on, there was the episode of the Jewish family living on the outskirts of town who got into trouble over black-market dealings in petrol. (One of them went to jail.) The remarks I heard at the time laid as much stress on their origins as their activities: I was reminded of them long afterwards, when I came across Lewis Namier's observation that 'it wasn't the black market that gave the Jews a bad name, it was the Jews who gave the black market a bad name'.

Such things shouldn't be minimised: they certainly set one on edge. Yet they were also surprisingly easy to put out of one's mind. They complicated life, but they didn't define it, and if I had been asked whether I felt at home in Egham, I would still have said – perhaps after a slight pause – yes.

6

Amusements

Adults lead divided lives. So, contrary to romantic myth, do children. If anything, an even deeper division runs through one's early years than one's later ones – between inner and outer worlds, between private thoughts or imaginings and the common currency of classroom, playground and street. An unrepeatable innocence coexists with scruffy experience.

The colours are brighter in childhood, the air is clearer. The roads not taken are more mysterious, and anticipations are more intense. That much of the romantic myth (and it is a great deal) is true. The world of my early years – like anyone's early world, I hope – was full of enchantments. A twig outlined against the sky, rain trickling down a window: things mattered, seemed momentous, simply because they were there.

But if I partly inhabited a magical domain, another part of me belonged at least in spirit to the world of Just William and Nigel Molesworth. Happiness took so many different forms. There were moments of absolute serenity or sudden exaltation. There were also funny faces and rude noises, inane greetings ('Look who it isn't!') and low-level nicknames, idiot wheezes and copycat jokes. There is no getting away from it, boys can be puerile. That's what puerile means.

I was neither an especially shy child nor a particularly gregarious one. I had no trouble striking up moderate friendships and I became adept at pretending to be more sociable than I felt: I was afraid of being thought stand-offish if I didn't. But I never had a Best Friend, and never joined a gang. It wasn't until I was fifteen or sixteen that I became genuinely close to anyone of my own age.

One great hazard of childhood I was largely spared. Bullying and intimidation were never my lot – not in any significant way, not even during my two years at boarding school. To have escaped them altogether would have been virtually impossible. There were one or two isolated incidents – arm-twistings, pinnings-down – and a classic episode in which a boy from another school threatened to 'get me' on my way home. (He was a stone-thrower, too: it was scary enough to make me take another route for a few days.) But in general I wasn't the kind of child whom other children picked on.

I would like to be able to claim that I was never among the ranks of the bullies myself, and I think I can say that this is *almost* true. But the memory of one small ugly affair ruffles my good conscience. I was roaming through the farmer's fields with my neighbour Bruce when a boy called Fuller whom we both knew slightly appeared from nowhere. He chatted to us for a minute, showed us his new catapult, and then suddenly ordered Bruce to start dancing round a cow-pat, shooting pebbles at his legs and warning him that there would be worse to come if he tried to stop. I didn't join in, but neither did I do anything to help; I simply stood by, until Fuller decided that he had had enough fun and wandered off.

Why didn't I intervene? It can hardly have been out of fear: we would have been two against one, and Fuller was quite a small boy. Strategically, too, it would have been the sensible course. I couldn't be sure that Fuller wasn't going to turn on me next, and by failing to ally myself with Bruce I was forfeiting any claim to his support. So what was it that held me back and kept me transfixed? I can't recall what I actually felt, but it is hard to believe that there wasn't a strong element of sadistic fascination. Something bad had been aroused in me, and my only consolation is that it seems to have been a unique incident. I have no other memories of the same kind.

One of the things which enabled me to feign more friendship with boys than I felt was the fact that I had my fair share, perfectly unfeigned, of standard schoolboy enthusiasms. Some of them were relatively short-lived, such as my Meccano phase (though it persisted long enough for me to build a cantilever bridge). My addiction to stamp collecting, on the other hand, lasted a good deal longer. It could partly, I suppose, be called educational: I picked up rather more than I would otherwise have done about national symbols, foreign currencies and the whereabouts of Tannu-Tuva and the Gilbert and Ellice Islands – to say nothing of the true identity of such mysterious-sounding places as Helvetia and Norge. There were crumbs of history to be gleaned, too: I pieced together a private Mount Rushmore of stamps portraying American presidents, everyone from George Washington to Rutherford B. Hayes. But the real appeal of stamps was aesthetic. I loved the microscopic artwork and the enticing colour variations (something Walter Benjamin has celebrated in one of his essays). I loved the colours themselves and the names under which they were listed in the catalogues – puce, lilac, salmon, sepia, orange red, steel blue. My actual collecting, I should add, was conducted on a very modest scale, through swapping and buying lucky-dip packets at the local stationer's. I didn't even acquire a decent album until I had been collecting for a year or so: I was setting out, none too cheerfully, for boarding school, when my father, on a sudden impulse, popped into a shop and bought me one. I felt an enormous surge of love for him; but within a couple of months I had given up collecting completely. There were boys at school who spent large sums on their collections (even the hinges had to be top-quality), and who contrived to be very tiresome about it. The spell was broken.

Of all my childhood enthusiasms, the strongest was for comics. I found my first encounter with them, in the persons of Mrs Bruin and Tiger Tim, only mildy enjoyable; but once I had discovered the *Beano* and the *Dandy*, Timberlake the newsagent (Timberlake himself was a dusty old man with Victorian side whiskers) became an Aladdin's cave. I used to rush round there once a week for the latest issues, and I was never disappointed. How could I have been, when Korky the Cat and Big Eggo and Desperate Dan were all waiting for me? Desperate Dan, as most readers will know, was in a class by himself, with a whole mythology clustering round him – Cactusville, Aunt Aggie, the cow pies with the horns left in.

But I was almost equally entranced by the lesser manikins who scampered across the succeeding pages – Keyhole Kate, Julius Caesar the Sneezing Caesar, a mini-Duce known (I fear) as Musso the Wop, Pansy Potter the Strong Man's Daughter, India-Rubber Ron. And then, when Dandyish and Beanoesque pleasures were exhausted, there were the real-life manikins of *Film Fun* and *Radio Fun* – fun with Arthur Askey in sepia, fun with Abbott and Costello in black and white. Of the two, *Radio Fun* was my favourite. For a time, unless I have dreamed it, it ran a strip inspired by the BBC programme *The Brains Trust*, with tiny representations of Julian Huxley, Professor Joad ('It all depends what you mean') and Commander Campbell pouring whitewash over one another and playing boisterous practical jokes.

Perhaps it is just as well that my parents didn't know about this last. They were always extremely indulgent about my reading comics, except on the occasion when they came across me reading one (not the *Beano* or the *Dandy* – I suspect it was *Comic Cuts*) featuring a character called the Potty Professor. They told me it was cheap and silly, and my father gave something close to a snort of disgust: anything ridiculing the life of scholarship was calcu-lated to earn his particular disapproval. But there was no subsequent attempt to censor my reading or institute a general ban.

Graduating from strip comics to comics which were largely text merely intensified my addiction. Many hours were now spent living in the fantasy world of the *Hotspur*, the *Wizard*, *Adventure*, the *Rover* and the *Champion*. The *Wizard* was much prized as the paper which featured the adventures of Wilson, the homespun elixir-drinking superman who emerged from the Yorkshire moors to break every conceivable athletic record. But for me the *Hotspur* was even more unmissable, because it was the home of a remarkable school, Red Circle. Who ever heard of a school with a name like that? But then who ever heard of a school with special houses for American boys ('Yank House') and boys from the colonies ('Conk House')? The central figure in the Red Circle saga, betraying the paper's Scottish origins, was a fourth-former called Rob Roy Macgregor, who could toss a well-directed caber when occasion demanded. But there were other memorable characters, too – Rob Roy's form master Alfred J. Smugg, for instance, and Chaka the Zulu Boy (an inmate of Conk House, needless to say) who knew how to hurl a mean assegai when there was no alternative.

None of the school stories in the *Hotspur*'s rivals quite came up to that. But the *Wizard* had a fine series about the ordeals of a scholarship boy at a public school, 'Smith of the Lower Third', and of how he came under the protection of a friendly prefect called 'Ape' Carew. (Carew's parents, anticipating the need for a nickname, had thoughtfully given him the initials A.P.E.) And in any case, school was only one setting employed by the comics. Other stories featured cavemen, cowboys, pipe-smoking detectives and witch doctors, along with rajahs, robots, spies and infernal machines, sometimes in bizarre conjunction. In one series, a gallant Pathan took on half the Afrika Korps armed only with a cricket bat ('clicky-ba'). Another, entitled 'There Was Once a Game Called Football', described the furtive rediscovery of the game in a bleak dystopian future: it had something of the pathos with which the rediscovery of Shakespeare is described in *Brave New World*.

Everything about the comics interested me. I loved it when their Christmas numbers appeared, with the letters making up their titles weighed down with snow. I used to pore over the publishing details at the bottom of their back pages, pondering on the contrasts between the Amalgamated Press and D.C. Thomson of Dundee, speculating about the distributors, Gordon and Gotch, who seemed to reach all corners of the Empire. And I was intrigued by the differences of flavour between individual publications. The *Champion* was especially striking in this respect. It had an unusually strong Hibernian and Caledonian and Canadian input. It was exceptionally sporty and hearty, in a manner which I would have dreaded in real life. But I lapped it up all the same – even Fireworks Flynn the Wizard Sports Master of Caribou College, who was portrayed in the introductory artwork sliding down the banisters on a tea tray. The most famous character in the comic was the pugilistic RAF pilot Rockfist Rogan, who thought nothing of engaging in fisticuffs standing on the wing of his plane in mid-air. It also ran a series about a Mountie called Lionheart

Logan; on the other hand you had to buy the *Rover* or *Adventure* if you wanted to follow the exploits of the football manager Baldy Hogan.

My childhood love of the cinema was almost as great as my passion for comics. It would probably have exceeded it if I had been able to go more often, although I wouldn't have been ready for half the films on offer: a full-blown addiction had to wait until I was entering my teens. But the seeds were sown much earlier.

First came the special outings – *The Wizard of Oz*, the early full-length Disneys, *Lassie Come Home*, horsy films such as *National Velvet* and *My Friend Flicka*, a visit with my father to *The Gold Rush*. I was an instant convert to Disney, and whatever one thinks about some of his later efforts, and about the progress of worldwide Disneyfication, nothing will persuade me that *Pinocchio*, *Dumbo* and *Bambi* aren't works of genius – or that Mickey Mouse and Donald Duck (whom I didn't get to know until a bit later) aren't creations of genius, either. Naturally you needed the cinema to appreciate them to the full, but I was able to linger over the graphic qualities which have made their images so durable in *Mickey Mouse Weekly*, a publication that seemed to hail from an altogether brighter and more streamlined world than any of my other comics (in effect, from the world of American design and technology). As for Chaplin, he is another master about whom I find it impossible not to have equivocal feelings. He is very out of fashion today, and I can see why, but I think his stock will rise again (though admittedly to a point well short of the height at which it once stood). I also think I was lucky to begin with one of his masterpieces. The cabin teetering on the edge of the precipice; the stalking bear; the starving hero dining on a boiled boot; the climb through the snowy pass; the party where nobody shows up – scene after scene in *The Gold Rush* captivated me and stayed with me. The occasion was all the more special because it was the first (and virtually the only) film my father took me to. He hardly ever went himself, though he rather liked newsreel theatres: he had a weakness for the 'shorts' featuring Robert Benchley, whimsical lectures on such topics as 'How to Sleep'.

Two other big occasions stand out. One was being taken to see *The Sea Wolf*, with Edward G. Robinson as the tyrannical

Captain Larsen. I found it enormously exciting (not least when Robinson quoted Milton's lines about it being better to reign in hell than serve in heaven), and for the first time I became fascinated by a star on his own account, not simply by the role he was playing. I resolved to see as many of Robinson's other films as I could, and began looking out for news items about him: it was a bonus to learn that his original name was Goldenberg. (Those members of my family who were film-goers took a lively interest in the Jewish aspects of Hollywood: we all knew, for example, that good-looking John Garfield – who was also in *The Sea Wolf* – had begun life as Garfinkle.)

The second landmark was Errol Flynn in *The Adventures of Robin Hood*. A glorious film; and this time I found myself hooked not only on the star, but on virtually all the leading members of the cast as well – on Basil Rathbone as Sir Guy of Gisborne, Claude Rains as Prince John, Alan Hale as Little John, Eugene Pallette as Friar Tuck ... (A cousin I saw soon afterwards on a visit to London had a book-of-the-film which enabled me to check up on who they were.) It was the first sign of the true addict's thirst for detail, and over the next year or two I extended the same passion to westerns, musicals, pirate films, and just about any celluloid confection that came my way. The screen conferred an aura on anyone who appeared on it, on supporting players no less than stars, and on the stars of second features and series (David Farrar as Sexton Blake, Cesar Romero as the Cisco Kid) quite as much as on the big names. One of my favourite actors in later years, for instance, was George Sanders. (Has there ever been a theatre critic as smooth and acidulous as the one he played in *All about Eve*?) But at the time I got as much joy out of watching Sanders' brother Tom Conway routing wrongdoers in the role of the Falcon.

A few years ago, incidentally, I learned that the Falcon had originally been played by Sanders: when bigger parts beckoned he was written out of the series, and brother Tom took over. The fact gave me a modest thrill, just as a thousand trivial facts about the films of my youth have in their time. All very pedantic, no doubt; but pedantry – caring about small things – can sometimes be a sign of love.

In the days before television, merely crossing the threshold of a cinema was an adventure. Whatever television's charms, having talking pictures on tap in your home isn't the same thing. So, too, with radio in my childhood. You couldn't get very excited about the medium itself: it was too commonplace. But that also meant that it was woven deep into the fabric of our lives. Like most of my contemporaries, or so I imagine, I was a BBC child in more ways than I will ever be able to calculate.

The programme which counted most was *Children's Hour*. I was avid for everything it had to offer: 'Toytown', 'Worzel Gummidge' (and his sweetheart Earthy Mangold), 'Norman and Henry Bones, Boy Detectives', even 'Cowleaze Farm'. I was intrigued by the curiously resonant names of some of the regular scriptwriters – S.G. Hulme Beaman, L. du Garde Peach – and enthralled by the serials: an adaptation of Stevenson's *The Black Arrow* was my effective introduction to historical fiction, *The Swish of the Curtain* first gave me the idea that the theatre might be (or might be thought to be) a glamorous way of life. And I relished the humour. There was one wonderful moment – it said so much about childhood – in a story about a small boy and his sister who somehow took part in the first rocket trip to the moon. On their return, there were cheering thousands waiting to greet them at the spacedrome: as the boy clambered out of the rocket, his mother gave him a hug and then murmured in his ear, 'You need a haircut.'

By today's standards *Children's Hour* was an almost impossibly polite programme. There was no jabbering, no jumping up and down. The presiding spirit was that of the producer, firm, sensible 'Uncle Mac' (Derek McCullough), and the closing note every night was that of his slightly grave farewell: 'Good night children' – a slight pause – 'everywhere.' It is a far cry from the world of Uncle Mac to that of the BBC children's television presenter who recently posed in the nude for a men's magazine, displaying a pierced nipple, or of her colleague on *Blue Peter* who lost his job after a prolonged trip on cocaine. *O earth, what changes hast thou seen.* It is only fair to add, however, that even at the time many listeners to *Children's Hour* felt the need for rowdier fare as well – for the *Beano* and the *Dandy*, as you might say. I rejoiced, too, years later, in the story of the evening when they forgot to switch off the microphone at the end of the programme, and Uncle Mac was heard to add, 'Well, that should keep the little buggers quiet for a bit.' But I still think there was something right and sound and deeply reassuring about that good-night message being sent out night after night, especially during the war years. It was all the more affecting when one learned (as I only did from his obituaries) that Derek McCullough had suffered fearful injuries as a soldier in the First World War – he had lost an eye, an arm and a lung; and it was pleasant to be reminded by the same obituaries that he had also found time to play the part of Larry the Lamb in 'Toytown'.

From early on, I strayed into the world of grown-up programmes as well, or simply found myself exposed to them. *Monday Night at Eight* came flowing into the living room, with 'this week's deliberate mistake'; so did *In Town Tonight*, with its opening sound-picture of the West End ('Read all about it!', 'Violets, lady, lovely violets'); so did *Workers' Playtime*, with a roar from the audience every time anyone mentioned the foreman. I was suitably gripped by the tales of the macabre introduced by 'your storyteller, the Man in Black'. I listened in to *Saturday Night Theatre*, and thought for a time that A.A. Milne's *The Truth About Blayds* had to be the cleverest play ever written. But it was comedians and comedy programmes that counted the most. My head was abuzz with catchphrases and signature tunes. So, it seemed, was almost everyone else's; and though I pass over the memory of a score of other entertainers with a pang, the programme I cherished most was the one which was also the best known, *ITMA*.

There are records of *ITMA* available, but I have avoided them: I am afraid they might prove too much of a disappointment. Better to smile at the memory of Colonel Chinstrap or Funf the German spy or Mona Lott, than to risk finding that one could no longer laugh at the actual gags. Where my faith remains firm, on the other hand, is in the warmth of Tommy Handley's personality, and in the surreal reality of the worlds he lorded it over, first as Minister of Aggravation, then as Mayor of Foaming-at-the-Mouth and finally as the last of the great proconsuls, the Governor of Tomtopia. The bold attack of the signature tune ('When trouble's brewing/It's his doing') put you right on Handley's side from the start; his fluency and easy manner did the rest. At the same time, few of the characters with which the programme swarmed seemed merely mechanical – or rather (since I have no doubt forgotten most of them), it is impressive how many of them, having begun as not much more than walking catchphrases, quickly took on a life of their own. They had such perfect names, too. Who could resist Frisby Dyke the bemused Liverpudlian, or Signor So-So, or the Hon. Mrs de Point? And there was something of the simplicity of genius in coming up with a Russian character called Vodkin.

It was from the BBC, too (since we didn't have a gramophone at the time), that I picked up almost all the popular music with which I was becoming saturated, without quite being aware of it. I certainly didn't make a conscious effort to learn songs. I was in my twenties before I began to realise how much I had absorbed, the words especially.

This was in sad contrast with my lack of response to learning the piano. Week after week I trudged across town for an hour's instruction with Mr Clayton, who also taught at a nearby private school. He was an elderly, frail-looking man, but he must have had a tough constitution to put up with me as patiently as he did. It wasn't that I actively resisted. I just didn't have the feel of the thing, and eventually the lessons were given up as a bad job. (My brother was to do far better when he studied the violin.)

While there is no logical connection, this failure became linked in my mind with my inadequate appreciation of classical music. Another sad contrast, or at any rate a troubling one. I only felt the greatness of the great classical composers intermittently. I had to school myself to respond to them as they deserved; in some respects I have never succeeded. But my heart went out instinctively to 'Spring Will Be a Little Late This Year' and 'Long Ago and Far Away'.

My immersion in popular culture went even further. I had an abiding fondness for advertising jingles, for example, even for the hopeless little rhymes on official wartime posters ('Billy Brown of London Town', 'Coughs and sneezes spread diseases'). And I took a voluptuous pleasure in the illustrations in magazines, provided they were glamorous enough or picturesque enough. A copy of the *Saturday Evening Post* which came my way kept me happy for hours, while I became a positive connoisseur of the pictures in my mother's copies of *Woman* and *Woman's Own*. An artist called Clixby Watson was my favourite: soft colours, suave backgrounds, romantic girls in angora sweaters.

Compared with this bombardment of mass-produced attractions, the deeper, more magical experiences of which I have spoken may sound insubstantial, mere glimpses and glimmerings. What they lacked in duration, however, they made up for in intensity. They were also oddly varied. Sometimes they were sudden reactions to a place or sight. Often they were the feelings produced by an unknown scene which swam up out of nowhere: light reflected on a sheet of water; children playing in a Japanese garden; a skyscraper overlooking a harbour. The power of such scenes lay in the curious sensation that they were simultaneously both strange and well loved. 'I have been here before.' And I *had* been there before, since they can only have had their origin in memories – in moments which had been preserved without one realising it, and then taken apart, transmuted and rearranged. An adult's imagination draws on a reservoir laid down in childhood. A child's imagination draws on earlier phases of childhood, and perhaps most abundantly (who can say?) on that earliest, prehistoric phase from which no conscious memories remain.

Two things were missing. One was anything which gave these disparate experiences a focus or framework. (No doubt religion should have done, but in my case at least it didn't.) The other was some means of expressing them. Not that I would have wanted to talk about them, even if I had been able to; least of all (I tremble at the thought) to other boys. But I did feel an obscure need to put them into words.

To find the right words – adequate words – was beyond me then, and it is beyond me today. I can only take refuge in some lines from D.J. Enright's sequence of poems about his childhood, *The Terrible Shears*:

> The happiness you must take as read,
> The writing of it is so difficult.

A wise strategy (even if Enright underrates his own abilities). Few things are more deadening than attempting to celebrate an emotion which you can't convey.

Fortunately, however, other people's words were at hand, to express the equivalent of what I felt, and far more; to provide, not exactly a framework for my thoughts, but a virtual second existence. Amid all the competing interests of life, I was being drawn slowly – and, as it turned out, irrevocably – towards literature.

7

Inspirations

Nursery rhymes, first. Fairy tales, too; but the nursery rhymes made the deeper impression. They seemed such pure distillations, so distinct and complete in themselves. You could no more imagine Miss Muffet on her tuffet eating bread and honey than you could imagine the queen in her parlour eating curds and whey. And the clarity of the images was matched by the seeming inevitability of the action. It was only natural that the Queen of Spain's daughter should come to visit whoever it was who had the little nut tree. It seemed a matter of course that the Man in the Moon, having tumbled down, should ask his way to Norwich, and equally right and proper – no mere consequence of the need for a rhyme – that the Man in the South should have been eating cold plum porridge. (What could have been more logical, either, than that he should have burned his mouth with it?)

Above all, nursery rhymes instil a feeling for rhythm, word-patterns and the shades and colours of language. Many of them are miniature masterpieces. (Anon can sometimes be as exquisite a craftsman as Tennyson or Pope.) They are also the seedbed of a love of poetry in later years, which makes it all the more depressing to read, as you sometimes do nowadays, of children who arrive at school unable to recite any. But perhaps such reports are scare stories, and wildly unrepresentative. Certainly one shouldn't underrate the tenacity which the rhymes have shown in the past. In an essay on Mother Goose, Maurice Sendak quotes from the pugnacious preface to an early nineteenth-century American edition, in which the old lady turns on her critics and rivals, and insists that her rhymes are as immortal as those of 'Billy Shakespeare':

No, no, my Melodies will never die,
While nurses sing, or babies cry.

Let us hope so.

After nursery rhymes, the first contact with poetry I can recall is some dismal chanting at my council school ('That's the way for Billy and me'). After that, there is a long blank – or would be, if it weren't for some of the songs we learned, which were as good as poems: 'Early One Morning', Bobby Shafto's silver buckles, the misty pathos at the end of 'D'ye ken John Peel?'. Of straight poetry, however, without benefit of music, nothing seems to have made any impression until I got to Mrs Gittins'.

Nothing I was taught, that is. But at some stage I had begun exploring for myself; and from then on what I learned at school was to mean a good deal less to me, with a few exceptions, than what I read at home. I am speaking only of literature, needless to say, not of other subjects. But then the whole point of one's own reading was that it wasn't a 'subject'. The only reason for picking up a book was because you wanted to.

I wasn't living in a vacuum, however. The course my reading took was shaped by what was available, by what I had heard about, by parental attitudes, often by pure chance. Looking back, I have come to think of all kinds of people as benefactors who steered me towards literature, however unknowingly or indirectly. Let me record my debt to four of them – only one of them someone I actually knew, and then only very slightly.

Miss Barnes was the English teacher at the grammar school at which my mother won a place when she was eleven. She remains a shadowy figure, but her lessons made an impression: the only school book which my mother had kept was an illustrated Nelson's Classics edition of *The Golden Treasury*, its endpapers and blank leaves covered with notes in her schoolgirl handwriting.

One day I picked it up. What attracted me in the first place were the brightly coloured illustrations. The frontispiece showed a girl in a blue dress bending over a guitar, with two lines underneath which I found instantly affecting:

> It keeps its highest holiest tone
> For one beloved Friend alone.

When I turned to the poem from which they came, however – Shelley's 'Ariel to Miranda' – I couldn't get much out of it; but I had better luck following up the next picture (which went with a poem by Walter Scott), a Maid Marian-ish girl in yellow standing on a castle wall singing about Brignall Banks and Greta woods:

> I'd rather rove with Edmund there
> Than reign our English queen.

Then came an illustration accompanying Wordsworth's 'Simon Lee the Old Huntsman', a poem which later on a comic anthology of bad verse was to encourage me to laugh at, especially the lines about poor old Simon's weak ankles, but which at the age of eight or nine moved me close to tears. (And are swollen ankles really such a joke?) Finally, a daub which would hardly have done for a cheap jigsaw directed me towards 'La Belle Dame sans Merci', and I knew even then that I had struck treasure.

Not long afterwards I picked up the book again. This time I began at the beginning; and there, waiting on the first page, was Drummond of Hawthornden:

> Phoebus, arise!
> And paint the sable skies
> With azure, white, and red:
> Rouse Memnon's mother from her Tithon's bed . . .

I was captivated as much as anything by the contrast between the short lines and the long ones. I was also puzzled by Memnon and Tithon; but I soon found out that Palgrave's explanatory notes were not only useful, but encouraging and reader-friendly. And after that I began exploring the book at will. It became my close companion.

My mother was an ardent novel-reader as a girl, so enthusiastic that she would sometimes run (literally) to the library, or so she has told me. *The Count of Monte Cristo* was a particular favourite – when I was young, she would try to recapture its excitements by solemnly intoning, 'To every man who sins comes NEMESIS'. She was also devoted to some of the more respectable best-sellers of the 1920s, and I have heard her musing with just the hint of a sigh on the neglect which has overtaken them. ('I don't suppose people read Sheila Kaye-Smith any more.') But the book which meant the most to her was beyond question *Vanity Fair*. Her Everyman edition was the only book from her schooldays apart from *The Golden Treasury* that she hadn't been able to part with. She has gone back to it again and again, and in her eighties the characters in it remain as real to her as though they were people she actually knew. She can't help taking Becky's part, in spite of everything; she feels sorry for Rawdon; she thinks of Thackeray himself as a friend.

When I first tried to read it myself I was too young, and I didn't tackle it again until years later. But I hadn't been put off, and I knew that I was bound to return to it one day. My mother had helped to persuade me that novels were fascinating worlds, even if I wasn't ready for them yet.

George Washington Kilner was someone whose name my father always mentioned with respect (and never without the 'Washington'). He had been appointed lecturer in English and Classics at Jews' College, the only non-Jew on the staff, back in 1881, so he was already a veteran of almost forty years' standing when my father attended his classes. He went on teaching at the college until 1935, combining his duties there with a lectureship at a college for Nonconformist ministers.

Kilner's lessons were the only formal instruction in English literature which my father ever received. They can't have been more than 'outlines', but they certainly succeeded in implanting information about some of the major figures – Bacon, Milton, Pope, Johnson, Goldsmith, Lamb, Macaulay (favoured for his essay and speech on 'Jewish Disablities'). No less important, from my own point of view, they instilled a respect for the whole idea of

English literature – or rather, since I think my father would have had that anyway, they put flesh on it. This made things much easier when the time eventually came for me to tell him that I wanted to study literature rather than medicine.

Kilner also fostered an enthusiasm, if only at a distance, for the classics. My father was very keen on me learning something about ancient history, and still more ancient legend, at an early stage. One of the first books he gave me, after I had graduated beyond picture books, was Charles Kingsley's *The Heroes*. Perseus and Andromeda, the Argonauts, Theseus and Ariadne: the stories weren't particularly easy reading, but they had a power (unlike Lamb's *Tales from Shakespeare*, given to me not long afterwards) which made me persist. Even more successful was a carefully chosen birthday present, a book about the myths of Greece and Rome, illustrated with reproductions of paintings (Victorian rather than Renaissance), and punctuated by brief quotations from English poetry. I remember staring at the words

> Jupiter
> Became a bull, and bellowed

as though they were some kind of mysterious gnomic utterance – an effect partly created by the fact that they were surrounded by lots of white space. And then there was the lesson which my father turned into a little game, quizzing me at odd moments about the Roman equivalents of Greek gods and heroes, and vice versa. (I always had trouble over Hephaestus.)

Although his knowledge of Greece and Rome may not have gone very deep (and he would never have pretended otherwise), no one who knew him could have doubted that the near reverence he felt for their achievements was sincere. Quite how much the idea of them meant to him was brought home to me by an incident towards the end of his life.

In 1958 I left for a year in America. My father had had a heart attack the year before, and though nobody said anything, the possibility that we might never see each other again was in our minds. So when, at a farewell party, one of my uncles produced a tape recorder and suggested I tape a message, it was the cue for something personal – or would have been, if my father hadn't immediately intervened with a request: 'Why don't you say a few words in Latin?' Like everyone else there, I was taken aback; my schoolboy Latin had already faded, and all I could think of on the spur of the moment was the opening of the second book of the *Aeneid*. *Infandum, regina, iubes renovare dolorem*: 'You command me, O Queen, to renew a grief too deep to be told.' It wasn't exactly appropriate; but my father seemed well satisfied.

Joe West – I met him once or twice – was a jack of all trades who had known my father for years: among other things, he taught him to drive a car. At the beginning of the war he was working for the publishing firm of George Newnes (once famous as the publishers of the *Strand Magazine* and *Tit-Bits*), and he persuaded my parents to buy me a multivolume encyclopaedia for children which they were producing, *Newnes' Pictorial Knowledge*. It was laid out, under various broad headings, as a narrative, and rightly or wrongly I thought it superior to the rival which most of my schoolboy contemporaries seemed to have, Arthur Mee's *Children's Encyclopaedia*. At all events, it was a work to which I kept returning.

The pictures were the prime attraction – original artwork, photographs, but above all pictures from the great repertoire of heroic portraits and history painting (nineteenth century, most of it). I pored over representations of Dante clutching his side while Beatrice walked past him, of Napoleon on board HMS *Bellerophon*, of Robert Bruce watching a spider and James Watt watching a steam kettle; over Van Dyck's 'Charles I on Horseback', and Sir Edward Poynter's doomed sentry at Pompeii ('Faithful unto Death'). I puzzled, too, over the curious name 'Rischgitz' which appeared alongside so many of the captions (it was a photographic agency). Most of these illustrations were quite small, but that only made the large ones seem more dramatic. There was a striking full-page picture of Beethoven lying on the ground in a forest glade, and another of a looming Ben Nevis under the heading 'Caledonia Stern and Wild'.

When I turned to the text, the historical section appealed to me most. The simplified version of history which it inculcated was no doubt one which every serious historian has been busy correcting for the past hundred years; but it at least had the virtue of providing a map of the terrain, a sense of chronology and a framework to which I could relate my other reading. Those were long-term gains: at the time I read the historical chapters simply for the sake of the story, and took them as they came.

There was less about literature in *Pictorial Knowledge*, but what there was gave me my first taste for literary history: it was satisfying to learn (before I had read a line by either of them) that Dryden's style was like a broadsword and Pope's style was like a rapier. And a mini-anthology at the end of the literature section expanded my poetic horizons, largely because it contained one or two early twentieth-century poems which were more modern than anything I had come across before. (*The Golden Treasury* only went up to Shelley and Keats.) I was particularly taken with Masefield's 'Cargoes'. A decorative border depicting quinquereme and galleon and dirty British coaster was a bonus, but it was the poem itself which thrilled me, especially the final stanza about the coaster: the phrase 'salt-caked smoke stack' seemed as bold as anything that Gerard Manley Hopkins was to do later on.

There was a large second-hand furniture store at the foot of Egham Hill. One day my mother bought a box of books there. (Possibly they had been thrown in with an item of furniture.) Most of them were inscribed with the firmly penned signature of the previous owner – 'E. Ritchie', or in some cases, with a strange formality, 'Emmanuel Ritchie Esq.'.

About half of them were volumes of Kipling – red limp-leather editions (the imperial redness seemed to go with the ruddiness of 'Rudyard'), probably published in the twenties. The verse spoke to me first: both the separate collections, and the poems which accompanied the stories. The prose was more difficult. I had the common experience of being baffled by the elliptical manner of the tales in *Puck of Pook's Hill* and *Rewards and Fairies* (which is not to say they didn't have their magic), and at the same time finding the poems sandwiched between them dazzlingly direct. It was a true poet, not a versifier, who wrote 'The Runes of Weland's

Sword', 'A Song to Mithras', 'A St Helena Lullaby'. And the poems in *The Jungle Book* were equally potent.

> Now Chil the Kite brings home the night
> That Mang the Bat sets free—

There were cadences that could haunt you for a lifetime. But in this case, unlike that of the Puck book, the tales themselves spoke without impediment. My favourite was 'Rikki-Tikki-Tavi', which is surely one of the world's great short stories. The war between the mongoose and the cobras was very real to me, and the more powerful because it played on a child's secret fears that there are threats against which his parents will be unable to protect him.

As for Kipling's politics, at that stage they passed me by. I *was*, I think, half aware that there was something uncomfortable about him, that he had a brutal side, but I associated him at least as much with feelings of tenderness: he was the man who could bring a lump to my throat with such things as the lament of the hunted-down seals in 'Lukannon' ('The Beaches of Lukannon – before the sealers came!'). Above all, or so it seemed to me then, he portrayed the world as an adventure waiting to be undertaken, a shining prospect. One of his poems opened with an invocation to 'The God of Fair Beginnings'. It was an idea, or a phrase, which I particularly cherished.

The Ritchie purchase, if I can call it that, offered only a few clues as to Ritchie's character. He had evidently been a dog lover: our acquisitions included *Thy Servant a Dog*, which must surely be Kipling's most embarrassing book, and a handsome anthology about dogs – I was much impressed by the leaves of tissue paper guarding the illustrations – entitled *The More I See of Men*. ('The more, said one, of men I see,/The more do dogs appeal to me.') Then there was a life of Sir Henry Segrave, the racing driver, which I read pretty well at one go: for a long time Segrave's exploits were better known to me than those of his more famous rival Malcolm Campbell. And hardly less gripping, to someone who had never been in an art gallery, there were half a dozen brief volumes from a turn-of-the-century series on great artists. They included studies of Fra Angelico, Raphael and Botticelli, but my

favourite was the one on Holman Hunt, and my favourite picture
the reproduction of Hunt's *The Depths of the Sea*: a mermaid
dragging down a naked mariner.

It was poetry which predominated, however. Longfellow: I
raced through *Hiawatha*, but got bogged down in *Tales of a
Wayside Inn*. A collected Wordsworth in off-putting double
columns: I closed it almost as soon as I had opened it, but not
before noting that the poem on page one had been written when
he was fourteen. (Only four or five years left for me to make my
own debut.) A selected Browning: daunting at first, though within
a year or two he was to be my foremost enthusiasm. *The Rubáiyát
of Omar Khayyám*: it is scarcely too much to say (it seems the
right metaphor) that I was intoxicated.

I loved the copy we had bought – the soft green velvety covers;
the shiny paper with one stanza to a page, surrounded by an
arabesque of leaves and tendrils, and a coloured illustration on the
facing page. As for the poem itself, I could recall whole chunks
without any effort; I revelled in its imagery and rhythms, and felt
that it expressed truths about life and death more fully than
anything I had read before. In a curious way I linked it to the Bible
– or perhaps it wasn't so curious, since an early stanza pointed me
in that direction:

> Now the New Year reviving old Desires,
> The thoughtful Soul to Solitude retires,
> Where the WHITE HAND OF MOSES on the Bough
> Puts out, and Jesus from the ground suspires.

Just the thing for a small boy in a solemn mood. I wasn't quite
certain what 'suspires' meant, and I wondered why Moses
qualified for capital letters and Jesus didn't. But I admired 'old
Khayyám' for being *thoughtful* about his decision to enjoy life
while he could, not merely rushing in, and I was stirred, later on in
the poem, by his courage in standing up to God.

Frank avowals of mortality – in poetry, at least – were very
much to my juvenile taste. So was the notion of Death the Leveller.
James Shirley's 'The glories of our blood and state' was one of my
Golden Treasury favourites; and although for a long time, as far

as I was concerned, the *Rubáiyát* remained in a class by itself, nothing held a higher place among the runners-up than Gray's *Elegy*. One Sunday not long after the war, by way of a family excursion, we drove over to the churchyard at Stoke Poges. On the way there, unprompted, I reeled off several stanzas of the *Elegy*. I think my parents were partly impressed, and partly amused, and possibly a little bit alarmed: it must have seemed a slightly morbid performance on the part of one so young.

I discovered some further uplifting gloom in a book belonging to my father – the only book of verse he owned (and one which I don't suppose he had ever opened). At some time in the thirties he had bought several volumes in the old Thinker's Library: he must have gone through a phase of feeling that he ought to give the critics of religion a hearing. Along with Ernst Haeckel's *The Riddle of the Universe*, which I struggled with for a few pages, they included a selection of poems by James Thomson, the author of *The City of Dreadful Night*. Picking it up, I was immediately intrigued by the frontispiece, a smudgy reproduction of Dürer's engraving *Melancholia*, and by the bleak caption underneath: 'The "Melencolia" that transcends all wit'. (There was the incidental mystery of the strange spelling 'Melencolia': it was as puzzling as the notice at Waterloo Station which said that all tickets had to be 'shewn' at the barrier.) Then I tried *The City of Dreadful Night* itself. It was too long for me, and in some respects too difficult, but it left me with an unforgettable impression of dark terraces, murky causeways, huge squares, deserted mansions, grandiose monuments. 'The City is of Night; perchance of Death' – and I was also left with a suspicion that it wasn't altogether unlike London.

Naturally I read children's books as well, though with far less sense of striking out on my own: the Babar or Alice or Just William I enjoyed were, so to speak, everyone else's too. At the same time many children's classics never came my way, and much of what I did read was run-of-the-mill.

It seems unfair to speak about such books quite so casually when I got so much out of them. Even the middling ones could sometimes have a powerful impact. But an extended tribute would soon degenerate into a catalogue, so let me ration myself to three fairly random examples.

I failed with *Tom Brown's Schooldays* (it was a case of 'no, but I saw the movie'), but that lesser Victorian public school classic *The Fifth Form at St Dominic's* won me over completely. There was one episode in particular, in which a boy was wrongly suspected of having stolen an examination paper and sent to Coventry for the rest of the term: it only took a few pages, but it seemed to go on for as long as Napoleon's retreat from Moscow. Among more modern writers, I was devoted to the historical novels of Geoffrey Trease. (Their underlying communistic message meant as little to me as Kipling's imperialism.) And though they were not nearly as good as Trease's, I gobbled down several historical tales by Herbert Strang. A scene in one of them which oppressed me with its brutality – the more so since it was meant to be justified – was an account of a bully getting his comeuppance by being rolled downhill in a barrel.

One reason why the Herbert Strang books were bought by parents and urged on boys by teachers was because they were published by Oxford, which also brought out a companion series of books for girls by Mrs Herbert Strang. I pictured the Strangs as an ideal married couple, sharing a cottage, comparing their day's work over tea. Many years later I discovered that 'Herbert Strang' was the pseudonym of two middle-aged men who had worked for Oxford University Press most of their lives. It turned out that they were Mrs Herbert Strang, too.

8

War All Around

'Don't you know there's a war on?' It is the dreariest of the catchphrases that come trailing out of my childhood – a question which answered itself, a reminder of something which nobody needed to be reminded of. War was all around. It seeped into every corner of life; it manifested itself in a hundred different ways every day of the week. And yet I am also struck, looking back, by the extent to which it *didn't* impinge on my own small world. Yes, I knew there was a war on, but much of the time I was only half aware of it.

Age explains a great deal. When I started reading the memoir by my Oxford contemporary George MacBeth, *A Child of the War*, I felt ashamed that my own response to the war had been so much more meagre than his; but I felt somewhat better when I recalled that in September 1939 he had been seven and I had been only four. That three-year gap made a vast difference. I have no recollection of the outbreak of war, and I remained in a kind of haze about its general course until I was eight or so. I have no recollection of the Battle of Britain, or of hearing the news of the German invasion of Russia or of Pearl Harbor. I *do* recall hearing about the Blitz while it was still in progress, but only in a disjointed fashion: it was chiefly brought home to me by seeing bomb damage on trips to London.

At the same time the vocabulary of war, in its Home Front aspects, was woven into our daily speech. The big war might be hard to grasp, but the small war of salvage drives and blackout material and Woolton pies was inescapable. Barely remembering pre-war conditions, I took for granted a landscape in which key buildings were camouflaged and you might suddenly come across sandbags or barbed wire. Like the other boys on the street, I played at being an 'airy-buzzer', sticking my arms out like wings, making propeller noises with my lips. And I have scores of other memories which are no less specific and distinct for being commonplace – finding a piece of shrapnel, seeing a barrage balloon tethered to the ground (it reminded me of Dumbo), watching a group of Italian prisoners of war with patches on their tunics.

The period partly lives on in my mind as an era of exhortations – 'Make Do and Mend', 'Dig for Victory', 'Holidays at Home'. Even a child could sense that under their forced jollity, most of them were rather dismal; and the occasional glimpse of America, in a film or magazine, provided a standard by which the prevailing greyness could be judged. (I remember gazing entranced – it may well have been in that same *Saturday Evening Post* I have already mentioned – at a full-page, full-colour photograph of a can of Libby's fruit.) Yet everyone ate adequately, and in spite of queues and shortages there were no really grim deprivations, or none that I could see. It was another reason why the war didn't press down too hard.

As for air raids, they were something that happened to other people. Egham seemed relatively safe, and London, to a small child, seemed a long way away. (I didn't realise that the blaze created by the worst raids on the capital was clearly visible from high ground nearby.)

Then, around the middle of the war, a Morrison shelter was installed in our living room – a big steel table, painted black, with wire mesh at the sides. In principle it brought the reality of war closer home, but at first I treated it as though it were a piece of playground equipment. One of my favourite games had been constructing nests or hideaways out of chairs and blankets. Unfortunately they had had a way of collapsing almost as soon as they were built, and I had given the idea up, but now I had a really solid lair at my disposal. My brother was becoming old enough to share it with me, too.

With the advent of flying bombs, the V-1s and V-2s, life took a more serious turn, and the shelter began to be put to the use for which it had been intended. The first V-1 hit London soon after D-Day. (It fell in a street in Mile End, not far from my father's surgery.) But the southern approaches to the city were now fully exposed, too, and in due course a shop in Egham High Street sustained a direct hit. It was a tobacconist's belonging to a Scotsman called Mackay who was killed outright. In the days that followed everyone in the town flocked to see the damage, myself included. But I can't pretend to have been particularly moved. I was just curious.

By this time, however, I did at least have some idea of what was happening in the world at large. The war was no longer an all-encompassing blur, and I can in fact pinpoint the moment at which my picture of it swam into focus. One summer afternoon in 1943 I came back from an outing to Staines to find Spring Avenue abuzz. Neighbours were hanging around in the street, and several houses were flying Union Jacks. There was great news: Mussolini had been overthrown. I took in what the adults were saying, as I never quite had before, and then listened carefully to a BBC bulletin, trying to get the facts straight. One result is that a name which has always loomed disproportionately large in my impressions of the war is that of Mussolini's successor, Marshal Badoglio.

Another consequence was that I began reading the papers, or at any rate the headlines and the opening bits of some of the main stories. (Until then almost the only thing that had interested me in them was 'The Arkubs', a comic strip in the News Chronicle about Mr and Mrs Noah who lived in Ararat Avenue with their son Japhet.) Eventually I was moved to produce a newspaper myself. I would get up early, listen to the seven o'clock news, and cover four small pages as quickly as I could with the principal items I had heard, along with one or two joke advertisements: the aim was to present the finished product to my mother before she heard the same stories on the eight o'clock news. Much of what I learned in this way was no doubt muddled, much of it no more than a question of picking up names. But previously, as far as I can recall, I had thought of the war simply as a condition of life, something which would go on and on until one day we won. Now it had begun to acquire a narrative.

The biggest story I ran in my pocket newspaper was D-Day: it called for a special edition. But then even the least news-conscious boy could hardly have missed the significance of what was going on. At school, Mrs Gittins made us all sing 'Hearts of Oak', 'to add something new to this wonderful year'; in the line about 'our soldiers, our sailors, our statesmen', she sensibly substituted 'airmen' for 'statesmen'. And though the immediate euphoria soon faded – the V-1s alone would have been enough to see to that – there was no mistaking the increased certainty that victory was on its way.

I spent part of the summer of 1944 at a holiday school on Exmoor, run by a woman called Naomi Birnberg. She was a member of a distinguished Anglo-Jewish family, the Bentwiches; after studying at Cambridge she had become Maynard Keynes's secretary (and persuaded herself that he was in love with her). That she was dedicated to her work at the summer school, I have no doubt, but as far as I was concerned she quickly established herself as a pain in the neck. I had asked my mother to send me my weekly copy of the *Hotspur*. The first issue arrived; but Naomi, as we were encouraged to call her, disapproved, and it was promptly taken away. Instead, I was given a copy of the local Exmoor classic, *Lorna Doone*, which I found unreadable. And this was meant to be a *holiday* school! It was my first contact, though not my last, with high-minded Cambridge intolerance.

In spite of this blow, I enjoyed myself at the school. I have happy memories of an excursion to the slopes of Dunkery Beacon; of a play about David and Goliath which we staged (I was a Philistine); of coming back from a day-long ramble with our hands and faces stained with berries. And the progress of the war, remote though Exmoor seemed, contributed to my general sense of excitement. Naomi had a son, a year or two older than me, called Benedict. We took to each other, and we used to study the maps which appeared in the paper each day showing the latest state of the war in Normandy. (When I arrived at the school, the Americans were still fighting their way down the Cherbourg Peninsula.) He also introduced me to the idea of fighting one's own wars with pencil and paper, drawing imaginary battle-zones and shading them in as the armies of one country – the goodies, presumably, though it was scarcely a moral issue – gradually overcame the armies of another. He was a clever boy, and I rather hero-worshipped him. I have never seen him again, though I sometimes read about him. In later life he became a solicitor, and is well known for championing left-wing causes.

Over the months that followed, my enthusiasm for private war games increased. The maps became more elaborate, the manoeuvres more complicated. There was a distinct element of following a game in my attitude to the real war, too. Take the Battle of the Bulge. I had no idea what the soldiers involved were actually going through, but I still shiver at the thought that I found it an exciting development: a match was more dramatic if the other side staged a comeback before going down to defeat. Of such is the world of nine-year-olds, when they aren't directly threatened themselves.

In April 1945 my mother managed to take my brother (now aged five) and myself to Bournemouth for a few days. It was the first family holiday since before the war, but it is chiefly memorable to me on two other counts. Throughout our stay, my right leg was a study in purple and yellow: I had been exploring a disused building just before we left home, and fallen through a gap in the floorboards. And a day or two after we arrived, President Roosevelt died. People are supposed to be able to remember exactly where they were when they heard about the assassination of President Kennedy, but my memories of hearing the news about Roosevelt are no less precise. It seemed devastating.

After that, a sense of everything going by in a rush – I've only a confused memory of details – and suddenly it was VE Day. Bonfires, bunting, 'Roll Out the Barrel' (the first popular tune I actively disliked); pictures of a floodlit St Paul's; Churchill and the royal family on the balcony at Buckingham Palace, and on another balcony in Piccadilly adorable Zoë Gail singing 'I'm Going to Get Lit Up When the Lights Go Up in London':

> You will find me on the tiles,
> You will find me wreathed in smiles,
> I'm going to get so lit up I'll be visible for miles . . .

There was no question of us going up to London ourselves: I had to be content with what I could hear on the radio, and then with being allowed to stand on the fringe of the crowd milling around in Egham High Street. Not long afterwards, however, I accompanied my mother on an expedition to the West End, and while we were going down Oxford Street, I saw a large poster (I think it was outside a newsreel theatre) showing a group of horribly emaciated figures – a photograph from Belsen. My mother told me not to look, and we hurried past.

I can't recall when I first became aware that the Second World War was also a war against the Jews. Very early on, at a guess; and the knowledge must have been reinforced in many ways I have forgotten, by remarks I overheard and references I came across in passing. It was all fairly vague, however, partly because the subject was one which my parents hardly ever referred to in my presence. They were anxious, no doubt, to protect me from disturbing thoughts, and in this they were largely successful. It is possible that growing up in the Nazi period helped to shape my character at levels I can't assess: an awareness, however muted, that there were powerful people who were hoping to hurt me must have made *some* difference. But I don't think I was particularly prey to conscious fears. The knowledge that there were powerful people who were fighting the Nazis made a difference, too – a decisive one.

Not long before the end of the war I stayed with cousins in London and went with them for a day or two to their school – an elementary school, a tougher place than anything I had encountered before. While there, I heard a story about a group of German soldiers kicking around a Jewish baby like a football. I was old enough to know that you couldn't believe every story you heard in the playground, but somehow I never doubted the truth of this one. I soon heard rumours of other atrocities; then came Belsen, and facts which were worse than any rumour, and more facts. The Nuremberg trials got under way. The figure 'six million' acquired a dreadful significance. Everyone knew about the Holocaust (though not, at that stage, by that name). Or did they?

It is hard, half a century on, to convey quite how things stood.

For ten or fifteen years after the war, the facts of the Holocaust were both known and not known, generally acknowledged and very inadequately absorbed. That they were deplored goes without saying, but they were also relegated to the outer regions of public awareness. There are reasons, good and bad, why this should have been so, and there were a multitude of exceptions. But anyone who thinks I am exaggerating need only consider how few books were devoted to the subject, long after scholarship and authorship might have been expected to catch up.

I was eighteen when my own miscellaneous thoughts and feelings about the Holocaust crystallised into a determination to find out more, to get a clearer picture. When I looked for a book which treated the Jewish catastrophe as a whole, however, there was none to be found – and this was in 1953, eight years after the end of the war. (The admirable Leon Poliakov had in fact brought out the first such study, *La Bréviaire de la haine*, in 1951, but it had not yet been translated.) Then, shortly afterwards, Gerald Reitlinger published his pioneering history, *The Final Solution*. I got hold of a copy as soon as I could, and the dismay with which I read it still left room for admiration – admiration both for the skill with which Reitlinger marshalled such complicated material, and for the fact that he wrote so well, in such clean, trenchant English.

I have often wished that I had had a chance to meet him. He sounds a most unusual man, and certainly not what one would have predicted if all one had known about him was his work on Nazism. He was a noted collector of ceramics, who left his collection to the Ashmolean; an authority on the history of the art market; a traveller, who wrote books about Persia and the remote Chinese province of Yunnan; a social figure, known to the friends he used to entertain at his house in Sussex as 'the Squire'; a character with a 1920s flavour, by the sound of it, fond of such things as *bouts-rimés* and dressing-up games. (There is an engaging sketch of him in the memoirs of his friend Anthony Powell.) He must have been about fifty when he decided to immerse himself in the horrors recorded in *The Final Solution*, and though his work has inevitably been overtaken by subsequent scholarship, he deserves to be better remembered than he is. I once spoke about him to the formidable Holocaust historian Lucy

Dawidowicz, and I was pleased when she told me how grateful she had been for his book when it first appeared.

By 1960 a great deal more material was becoming available. I began reviewing around that time, and once they knew of my interest (although they could certainly have found writers with far more expertise), literary editors started sending me books by Holocaust survivors, including such major works as Primo Levi's memoirs and Chaim Kaplan's *Scroll of Agony*. I read lots of other books and articles on the subject as well, and I have continued to do so. Only intermittently, I should add: sustained exposure to such matters would be too much of a strain. But there have been very few days when I haven't thought about them.

It may seem as though I am running well beyond the limits of a childhood memoir; but knowledge of the Holocaust has modified, as nothing else has, what I feel about my childhood in retrospect. It is impossible not to reflect, if only from time to time, on how different things might have been. It is impossible not to think of myself as one of the lucky ones. I am Jewish, I had a happy childhood, as childhoods go, and I grew up during a period in which at every moment the most terrible things were being done to other Jewish children. It would be an exaggeration to say that the contrast makes me feel guilty; but it does sometimes make me feel numb.

There are many pitfalls in talking or even thinking about the Holocaust. One of them is the temptation to identify oneself more closely with the victims than one has any right to. It is a way of inflating one's own importance; at worst, of claiming some of the moral privileges of martyrdom. I can recall the writer T.R. Fyvel once saying to me, of a mutual acquaintance, 'The trouble with X is that he has never *quite* learned the difference between what happened at ABC [X's public school, where he had undoubtedly suffered from anti-Semitism] and what went on in the camps.' It may sound a harsh joke, but having encountered X's histrionics I knew what he meant. On the other hand I have more than once seen behaviour like that used as an excuse (though emphatically not by Fyvel) for dropping or downgrading the whole subject – just as in the fifties I was sometimes told that it was time to start forgetting the Holocaust by people who had plainly never begun to remember it.

Early on, I became aware that there was a difficult balance to be struck. The sense of affinity with the murdered millions ran deep; the gulf in terms of experience was immeasurable. With my father, it was naturally different. He, too, was one of 'the lucky ones', but he had spent his childhood in the midst of the world that had been destroyed. Most of the Jews in the area of Volhynia he came from, who had already suffered horribly, were massacred in the course of three or four days at the beginning of September 1942. In Gorokhov, where 2,500 were killed (out of a community of 3,000), a group of women were first tormented in various ways, including being forced to dance around while *Sifrei Torah* – Scrolls of the Law – were burned in the street. My grandmother was seventy at the time; if she hadn't emigrated, she might well have been one of them.

My father seldom spoke about the Holocaust directly. Long after his death, when my mother remarked to me one day, 'You know, he took it very badly' (without having to explain what 'it' was), I felt a slight shock. And yet I don't know why I should have done. When he *did* speak about it, his strength of feeling was clear; and it could easily be deduced from his comments on related topics – the fate of Yiddish, for example – and from oblique allusions.

He probably opened up more readily with contemporaries, or those who shared a similar background. One such, I suspect, was a rabbi to whom he felt particularly close, Yehoishue Szpetman. Not that there was anything especially lachrymose about Szpetman. He stays in my mind as a wiry, energetic figure, for ever on the go. But he was very much someone from the Old Country. He had come to London from Poland around 1920, and spent the rest of his career as rabbi of the Berditshever Shul, a synagogue in White-chapel. He was not only a Yiddish speaker but an ardent champion of the language, preaching his sermons in Yiddish and publishing some of them as a series of pamphlets. My father lit up in his presence; to me, on the other hand, he was necessarily far more remote. I can't recall us ever exchanging a word, beyond bare greetings. But he gave me a handsome Haggadah (a book containing the order of the Passover service) for my bar mitzvah.

Inside it he wrote a sprawling Hebrew inscription, which I couldn't make out; but the gift itself plainly implied that I was the repository of traditional hopes.

In Poland, Szpetman had been a friend of the Yiddish writer Hillel Zeitlin, and they had remained in touch. When I learned this, I realised the probable reason for my father's interest in Zeitlin, or at any rate for his first having come to read him. Later on, I read one or two of his essays myself, in English. They were more like parables – poetic, intense, shot through with a belief in the mission of the Jews to be a 'light to the nations', and with sadness at its non-fulfilment. I have also read an account of his eventual fate. In September 1942, during a major deportation of Jews from Warsaw, the Germans seized a Jewish hospital, where he was a patient. In common with the other patients, he was given five minutes to collect his belongings, and he found time to put on *tefillin* and a prayer shawl. According to an eyewitness, his demeanour as the group were herded away impressed everyone, even the Ukrainian militia: they refrained from shoving him along with their usual brutality. But this wasn't enough to save him from being sent to Treblinka and gassed on arrival.

There is a sketch by the Yiddish novelist Sholem Asch called *Triumphal March*, in which he imagines the slaughtered Jews of Warsaw restored to life and marching through the streets of the city: at the head of the column of religious writers he visualises Hillel Zeitlin, with 'his red-grey hair, his noble features, his red beard and his dreamy eyes always staring far away into hidden worlds'. The piece doesn't rise to as high a literary level as one might hope – it is poster-art – but I find it moving, even so. It enshrines not so much the wish to undo history, as the momentary belief that this particular piece of history could never have happened; that it is simply a bad dream, which is going to go away. And that is surely a feeling which we can all recognise.

9

A Cambridge Interlude

One morning in August 1945 I overslept. My father, who had come down to stay with us the previous evening, woke me up, impatient to tell me the news. The Americans had dropped an enormous bomb on Japan, much bigger than any bomb there had ever been before. The war would be over very soon.

This was my second big dramatic moment in the space of less than two weeks. Ten days earlier, on what was virtually my last day at her school, Mrs Gittins had gone up to her study, 'The Den', to listen to the General Election results on the BBC. An hour or so later she re-emerged; as she came slowly downstairs she announced to the faithful Mrs Chater, whom she had left in charge of her class: 'My dear, they've won.'

We were entering a new age, but its public portents and landmarks meant less to me than the fact that in September I was due to start at the local grammar school, Strode's – my first 'big' school. I was half-excited, half-apprehensive, and when the day came, it was as daunting as I had feared. Within half an hour I had lost my new fountain pen (a Swan) and got into a panic.

Quite soon, however, I had begun to find my way around, and a few memories stand out. There was a pretty red-haired French teacher called Miss Barnes and a no-nonsense middle-aged English teacher called Miss Bunn. (Most of the male members of the staff were still away in the Forces.) At Christmas I was moved, though not without a twinge of Jewish unease, when a teacher took us through the Latin of *Stabat mater* and the Middle English of 'I sing of a maiden that is makeles'. But on the whole the year which

I spent at the school made curiously little impression – largely, I
think, because I knew that I wasn't going to be there for very long.
I was looking forward to getting back to London.

I was also learning some of the joys of gregariousness. I became
an ardent Boy Scout, and it was undoubtedly the friendliness of
the movement which appealed to me more than anything else. For
a few months, I lived in a world of lanyards and woggles and
Tenderfoot badges. I honed my memory on 'Kim's Game', and
tied knots, incompetently; I went to camp, and joined in such
rousing chants as 'When he went to camp he had to fill 'is dixie, fill
'is dixie, fill 'is dixie'. (Phyllis Dixey, I should perhaps explain, was
the foremost striptease artiste of the day, famous for her show
Peek a Boo.) And then my interest faded, as suddenly as it had
dawned, and I dropped out.

A much longer lasting enthusiasm was for cricket. I was a
hopeless player, alas: my batting was an embarrassment, and I was
usually sent out to field in the longest of the long grass. But that
simply meant that my devotion had to find other outlets. I became
an accomplished scorer: the 'M' with which I used to join up the
dots after a maiden over was a little work of art. I proclaimed my
support for Surrey, and cheered on the emergence in that first post-
war season of Alec Bedser. Laurie Fishlock was another great
name at the Oval in those days; but then every leading player was
a hero as far as I was concerned, irrespective of his county. Walter
Hammond? A rock of reassurance. Hutton, Compton, Trevor
Bailey? Giants among men. And then there were their no less
illustrious predecessors. A boy I was friendly with lent me a book
on cricket between the wars by Sir Pelham Warner, and I soon had
dozens of new names to savour: Hendren, Maurice Tate, Frank
Wooley, the Nawab of Pataudi ... An especially golden aura
clung to the memory of Hedley Verity, who had been killed in the
war. And as for Jack Hobbs, the idea that he was now running a
shop in Fleet Street was like something out of Greek mythology, a
god assuming the shape of a mortal.

I was ruefully aware that all this was cricket at one remove, that
fate had aligned me with the followers of the game rather than the
performers. There was a cartoon in *Punch* which amused me: it
showed a tough-looking boy with a bat standing in front of an

improvised wicket, and a bespectacled, bookish-looking boy saying to him, 'No, you be Len Hutton and I'll be Neville Cardus.' (Cardus, I should again perhaps explain, was a cricket writer – some would say the best there has ever been.) Yet any kind of enthusiasm for cricket, even a bookish one, constituted a powerful bond with my schoolboy contemporaries.

The same year saw a turning inward as well as a turning outward. If I was now in some respects more of an extrovert, I also became more addicted to daydreaming and private games. (The imaginary wars and imaginary maps were duly supplemented by imaginary cricket matches.)

There is a wonderful passage about daydreams by the seventeenth-century divine, Jeremy Taylor. Taylor himself disapproved of them, although the warmth of his account makes it is hard to believe that he hadn't indulged in them as well:

> Some phantastick spirits will walk alone, and dream waking, of greatnesses, of palaces, of excellent orations, full theatres, loud applauses, sudden advancement, great fortunes; and so will spend an hour with imaginative pleasure, all their employment being nothing but fumes of pride, and secret, indefinite desires, and significations of what their heart wishes.

There are other kinds of daydream, no doubt, but Taylor was surely right to suggest that power and glory are the fantasist's commonest themes. Certainly my own adolescent flights of fancy were firmly in the Walter Mitty tradition. It wasn't enough for me to mastermind those imaginary games of cricket, for instance; I also had to picture myself taking part in them and performing amazing feats. This particular fantasy, as far as I can recall, came to full flower during the Australian tour of 1948. In the course of that season, though they may not have been aware of it, I punished Lindwall's bowling with almost frightening ferocity, scored 23 in a single over off Keith Miller (a full 36 would have been implausible), and caught Bradman in the slips. Nor was this all. Between matches I somehow managed to take part in the 1948

Olympics, and broke several records. As a sporting prodigy I was second only to Wilson of the *Wizard*.

By this time I was at school in Cambridge (where I was able to see the Australians play – in reality – at Fenners). I had been disappointed at being sent to the Perse, instead of going back to London, as I had expected, and there were many things I disliked about the place once I got there. Some were endemic to boarding-school life: the lack of privacy, the petty regulations. Others were a consequence of spartan post-war conditions. The food was often vile, none of it viler than the dehydrated egg – 'yellow peril' – with which we were frequently compelled to start the day. The harsh winter of 1946–7 and the accompanying fuel crisis left me with my hands covered with chilblains. Still, it could all have been far worse. Discipline was relatively mild, bullying was no more than a minor hazard. And there were compensations, or at any rate consolations – new scenes and new interests.

I began, indeed, on a note of high excitement. On my first evening at the school, an older boy gathered a group of new boys around him and gave us a *tour d'horizon* of his knowledge of sex. (We were eleven-year-olds, he must have been fourteen or fifteen.) It had the happy effect, although that can hardly have been his main purpose, of driving any thoughts of homesickness out of our minds, but in spite of his impressive manner it also proved to be a mine of misinformation. The most striking piece of advice which I carried away was that you could tell whether a woman was a prostitute by the fact that, if she was, she would be wearing a bangle – even when she was off duty, presumably – around her left ankle. For weeks afterwards I became a dedicated junior voyeur, casting furtive and fortunately undetected glances at women's ankles in shops and at bus stops. It was a quest which led nowhere.

Sex was still a Dark Continent. The coastline had been only imperfectly mapped, and the interior remained the subject of fantastic rumours. At the same time, there was so much in the way it was spoken about, or *not* spoken about, which conspired to make one think of it as a dirty business. I remember being puzzled by the slogan on the wartime posters warning against the dangers of VD: 'Clean Living is the Only Real Safeguard'. What exactly was VD? Even more of a mystery, what exactly did they mean by 'clean living'?

It is true that I had taken the Boy Scout oath to be 'clean in thought, word and deed', but at the time I hadn't been able to work out what that was all about, either. Then, shortly before I left Strode's, a boy who lived nearby not only explained the general theory of masturbation but kindly offered to demonstrate. He didn't, as it happened, complete the performance, but while it lasted he looked decidedly shifty. This was no innocent pleasure – not, at least, if you were to judge by his attitude.

A paradox began to take shape in my mind, though I couldn't have put it into words. I believed in romance, especially as purveyed by the cinema. (I wasn't one of those small boys who yawned or groaned in an action film when the action was held up by the love interest.) I also knew enough to know that romance presupposed sex. But sex, on the available evidence, seemed thoroughly unromantic.

I can't pretend that at eleven or twelve I was especially agitated by the contradiction, however – and meanwhile, my addiction to the movies, romance included, grew steadily stronger. There were less opportunities for indulging it as a boarder than there had been at home (something for which I envied the majority of my Perse classmates, who were day boys), but that only made those that there were seem more precious. I explored the resources of Cambridge, whenever I could, from the big picture houses in the centre of town to an out-of-bounds fleapit in Mill Road where most of the films they showed were leftovers from the thirties. (Oh, the joy of sneaking off there to see Ronald Colman in *The Man Who Broke the Bank at Monte Carlo*!) During the holidays – we were now back in London – I felt entitled to pop along to the Odeon or the ABC twice as often as I might otherwise have done, to make up for lost ground at school. And there was a fresh source of diversion. Our new next-door neighbours in Mile End were faithful readers of *Picturegoer*, and similar magazines; borrowing their copies, I was now able to comb through cast lists at leisure, down to the bittiest bit player in the flimsiest supporting feature.

I was learning about better films, too. Roger Manvell's book *Film* (a bible for my generation) steered me towards the big highbrow names. I saw my first French films at the Arts Cinema in Cambridge, and my first Italian ones at the Academy in Oxford Street, and didn't need to be told how far they outclassed the average Hollywood product. I was wild about Carol Reed's *Odd Man Out* and David Lean's *Great Expectations*. But my tastes remained, to put it mildly, eclectic. I was fascinated by James Mason in *Odd Man Out*, for instance, but I was no less fascinated by him in the melodramatics of *The Man in Grey* and *The Wicked Lady* and in the rich kitsch of *The Seventh Veil*. I was fascinated by him, full stop. At one point, during the school holidays, I wrote to the studio asking whether I could have a photograph of him (it was duly supplied), and also asking whether it could be sent to Hillel House, The Perse School, Cambridge, marked 'To Await Arrival'. It was a way of ensuring that there would be at least one item to look forward to at the beginning of the next term.

There was nothing special about my enthusiasm for films. Most of the boys shared it; one or two of them were far more deeply versed in cinema lore. If I stood out in any way, it was for my love of poetry – which was tolerated provided I didn't make too much of it – and for being good at 'English', which in at least one respect I was able to put to sound practical use. I had a facility for writing essays, they were a standard form of punishment, and I was happy to take on another boy's burden for a consideration – which at a time when food rationing was still in force meant above all for sweets or chocolate. The promise of a Mars bar, and I would knock off some reflections on 'Manners Maketh Man'; a couple of KitKats, and I was good for three or four sides on 'Punctuality is the Politeness of Kings'.

My new literary love, meanwhile, was Keats. I bought a pocket edition, edited by Palgrave, and kept coming back to it; I wrote solemn notes in the margin; I found a peculiar charm in the vignette on the title page – a woodcut of an antique shepherd playing a flute. I had also fallen under the spell of another writer, though in his case 'love' wasn't the right word. In 1946, Penguin Books celebrated the ninetieth birthday of Bernard Shaw by issuing ten of his books simultaneously, in first printings of 100,000 apiece. (It is hard to imagine now, but people queued up for them.) Two or three of these paperbacks, purchased with pocket money, marked the beginning of my Shaw Phase. There was something unendearing about him, even then, but he was amusing and challenging, and he seemed unstoppably clever. Above all, I was amazed that someone so old was still extant, and still writing: it was as though Robert Louis Stevenson were living down the road. Fired by the thought, for the first and last time in my life, I set about trying to get hold of an autograph, though without avowing my purpose. Instead, I sent a postcard to Ayot St Lawrence fearlessly outlining a few of my objections to the arguments in *The Black Girl in Search of Her God* (or possibly it was the preface to *Androcles and the Lion*). I was hoping to get one of the famous Shaw postcards in return; naturally I didn't.

Ancient though he was, Shaw also seemed to me, at the age of twelve, strikingly modern. He was the most radical major writer I had so far encountered. As yet, I had no idea that there were subsequent and more profound forms of literary modernism: the full realisation still lay two or three years ahead. But it was during my time at the Perse that the first rumours began to reach me.

The master who had taken over at Hillel House just before I arrived there also taught English. He was an intelligent man, well-intentioned and devoted to his subject. Unfortunately, he had a damp, dispiriting manner – a cruel schoolboy nickname to that effect was quickly fastened on to him – and he found it hard to impose his authority either as housemaster or in class. But he did take a decision for which I will always be grateful. For a term or two, one of the textbooks we used in English was the splendid anthology edited by W.H. Auden and John Garrett, *The Poet's Tongue*. It was a revelation, the big step forward from *The Golden Treasury*. The principal lesson which I learned from it, as I was meant to, was that poetry didn't have to be conventionally poetic, that it embraced sea shanties and clerihews and 'The Akond of Swat'. But Auden and Garrett also offered examples of verse in strange styles which I had never encountered before, though I could see that they were 'modern'. The one which dazzled me was by Edith Sitwell, the 'Tango-Pasodoble' ('When Don Pasquito arrived at the seaside') from *Façade*. The rhymes and rhythms were intoxicating; the images (the vanilla-coloured ladies, the hotels that 'bode of dreamless ease') seemed to open a window on to Paradise.

My devotion to *The Poet's Tongue* was responsible for an incident which was tiny enough in itself, but which made a sharp impression. There was an art master at the Perse called Crouch, bohemian in appearance but conventional in his tastes. One day he told us to draw a scene based on a poem we had read. The poem I chose was one I had found in the anthology, Vachell Lindsay's 'The Congo' – rousing stuff (though nowadays it is frowned on by the politically correct). Crouch, who had never heard of it, asked me to tell him something about it, and then said with a sneer, 'Modern, is it? I suppose it is by W.H. Auden or someone like that.' Up to that moment I had thought of Auden simply as one of the editors of *The Poet's Tongue*. Now I made a mental note – for future use, so to speak – that he was also a poet.

Another early brush with modernism struck an earthier note. Some of the older boys in Hillel House had got hold of a copy of *Ulysses*, and one of them showed me a few of what seemed to him the highlights, beginning with a couplet in the Nighttown episode:

> Moses, Moses, king of the jews,
> Wiped his arse in the Daily News.

I was startled. In 1947 this wasn't the kind of language, or sentiment, which you expected to find set down in print. And though the lines were plainly 'non-Jewish' (no Jew would have spoken of Moses as a king – he was always 'Moshe Rabbenu', Moses our Teacher), that didn't make their dragging down of a sacred figure, the most important figure in Judaism, seem any less shocking. It began to look as though one of the characteristics of *truly* modern literature was that nothing was safe in its presence.

Yet I didn't confuse the irreverent lines, or whoever was meant to be speaking them (it is 'A Voice from the Gallery'), with *Ulysses* itself. Dipping into it, before the other boys took it back, I was bewildered, as well I might have been, but also intrigued and obscurely stirred. Something was going on in it – something very much more than the 'dirty book' aspect – which I wanted to find out about. I wasn't ready for it yet, but neither did I forget it. I knew that there was a world there waiting to be explored.*

I enjoyed wandering around Cambridge. The university made little impression in itself, but as a backdrop it added enormously to a general sense of picturesqueness, a feeling I sometimes had of being inside a film, or a novel, or a film *of* a novel (*Great Expectations*, perhaps). Heffer's bookshop in Petty Cury, where no one seemed to object to prolonged browsing, was a favourite port of call, though I liked the market square even more – the stalls lit by flares selling cheap sweets, the stalls selling comics, and right in the middle, with a large sign proclaiming that we were a multicultural society even then, the stall belonging to Grodzinski the Jewish baker. The comic stalls were particularly alluring, because they sold American imports: comic books which I hadn't seen before – Spiderman, Mandrake the Magician, Captain Marvel, Captain Marvel Junior – along with American science fiction and horror magazines. Some of these last were really shoddy, but you never know what you are going to come across. All I recall of them now is that in one story, someone quoted some tremendous lines from a play which at that stage I hadn't read and knew very little about:

> In the most high and palmy state of Rome,
> A little ere the mightiest Julius fell,
> The graves stood tenantless, and the sheeted dead
> Did squeak and gibber in the Roman streets.

I am rather suprised, looking back, that the editor of a ten-cent magazine let such a recondite passage pass, but no doubt he thought that it was gruesome enough to get away with.

My interest in American comics was reinforced by the fact that the *Daily Express* was now serialising the 'Steve Canyon' strip. I

---

* I admire the French translators of *Ulysses*, incidentally, for the neat solution they hit on in their rendering of the offending couplet:

> Moïse, le roi d'Israël,
> S'torchait avec le *Daily Mail.*

admired the draughtsmanship, and started trying to draw a similar strip, purely for my own consumption. I even modelled my cartoon signature on that of Milton Caniff, Steve Canyon's creator. And my enthusiasm for cartooning found another outlet in endless doodling. I drew hundreds of faces – almost always men – and tried to imagine what kind of characters they belonged to. (It was a game which had been played to perfection by Turgenev, as I learned long afterwards when someone published a collection of his caricatures and the accompanying notes.)

At school, I wasn't doing as well as I should have done. The Perse had a high reputation. In the early years of the century it had had a celebrated headmaster, W.H.D. Rouse, editor of the Loeb Classical Library and pioneer of the 'Direct Method' of teaching Latin and Greek. (He was still alive during my time there, though very old.) It also had a strong tradition of encouraging music and drama, with a specially built theatre known, quaintly enough, as 'The Mummery'. The annual recitation prize was a big event: in my first year it was won by a boy with obvious theatrical gifts called Peter Hall. The atmosphere, by the standards of the time, was tolerant. But I found it hard to settle down.

Hillel House, situated on the outskirts of town, a couple of miles from the main school, was a world within a world. (There was a non-Jewish boarding house nearby, with an exceptionally lively housemaster, but we had only limited contacts.) I got on well enough with most of the other boys in the house. I picked up a good deal of Anglo-Jewish folklore from them, and learned about Jewish life outside London and the South: many of them came from the provinces, some of them from towns with minuscule Jewish communities such as Derby and Grimsby. The only boy I positively disliked was a prefect who went in for a certain amount of ear-tweaking and the like, and who was fond of proclaiming that he was 'a cynic' – and even he didn't trouble me unduly. On the other hand I still didn't have a best friend. I might have done, if I had been a bit older. One of the senior boys, Stanley Price, became a fast friend when we met up again some ten years later (by which time he had begun his career as a writer), and he has remained one ever since. But at school the age gap between us was too great.

I can't say I was exactly unhappy at the Perse: it would be too dramatic a word. But at the start of my second year I began to feel increasingly fed up, and in the winter term things grew worse. (A particular source of discontent was 'The Triangle', a cross-country run we were sent out on every weekend: if we failed to complete it on time, we were made to go through it all over again.) I felt weighed down: I longed for the London life which I had begun to have a taste of during the holidays. Then one day I was walking back from the school to Hillel House when it occurred to me that I had enough money on me for a ticket to Liverpool Street, and a little left over for the Underground. 'To hell with it': I went straight to the station, and within a couple of hours I was home. My parents were naturally worried when I showed up, but once they had established that there was nothing seriously wrong they agreed to take me away, provided I went back for the remainder of the school year, and provided the headmaster agreed that it was the best course. Which he did, and that was that.

With a release date in sight, my last months in the school passed easily. Towards the end of my time there, I had moments when I felt almost sentimental about the place, with a kind of premature nostalgia. At the very end, for a day or two, I succumbed to what I can only call a sense of mortality, a sad awareness that childhood was slipping away, along with a sudden romantic yearning for a boy of roughly my own age. (He was a boy in another class, whom I had barely noticed before.) A strange mood. But it soon melted away, and I began to wonder what London held in store.

10

East End Days

The East End to which we returned after the war had been bombed and scarred. It had also lost a good deal of its Jewish character. Even in 1939, the Jewish population was already only half what it had been at its peak, and since then, thanks to the Blitz and the wartime exodus, it had halved again. Yet if the old Jewish East End was plainly doomed, it took a long time dying. For another twenty years or so, until the 1960s, shops, businesses, markets and communal institutions gave the area a Jewish colouring which numbers alone no longer warranted.

It was largely on this account that it seemed to me, as we settled in, not so much a neighbourhood as a separate world. But the non-Jewish East End had its own special flavour as well, its own history and traditions; and my sense of the whole area as a place set apart was heightened by the fact that most outsiders had only a very vague idea of what life there was like. A fairly lurid idea, too, shaped to a considerable extent by journalistic legend (opium dens in Limehouse and all that). I had classmates at the City of London, boys from suburban Bromley or Petts Wood, for whom the mere fact that I went home every day to Mile End made me an object of interest, almost as though I had stepped out of the pages of a thriller.

It was when you approached the East End from the west, through the City, that its exotic quality was most apparent. 'Aldgate East, all get out!' was the joke cry on the Underground. But when he emerged, the visitor found that a mere three or four hundred yards had already carried him deep into unfamiliar territory. The traditional divide was back at Aldgate Pump, where Leadenhall Street and Fenchurch Street converged. The true one, if we are to be precise, was a little further on, where the short strip of Aldgate High Street began. On the left, St Botolph's Aldgate, the most easterly and dullest of City churches. On the right, an almighty London tangle, with a bus station, and the ancient Hoop and Grapes, and in between, guarding the portals of the east, a shop with a big red neon sign proclaiming 'Max Cohen Tailor'.

Every big city has its dramatic juxtapositions, but few can have been more dramatic than this one. It was strange to stand in an alley in Spitalfields, or to pass by the police station in Leman Street (which led down to the docks) or the little synagogue in Sandys Row, and to reflect that you had only just left behind the world of brokers and bankers and jobbers, that Lloyd's and the Baltic Exchange were only a short walk away. The break wasn't absolute: there was an intermediate zone around Houndsditch which was not quite the City (though it still was technically) and not quite the East End. But a few yards beyond you were drawn into an unmistakable East End world of workshops and small houses, and in no time at all you were in Middlesex Street itself, or Petticoat Lane, as it was still known long after its official change of name, though I never heard anyone call it that, either: it was always just 'the Lane'. (A friend and I once improvised a Jewish nursery rhyme about 'the little boy who lives down the Lane'. I can't remember now what the three bags full were full of.)

The East End was emphatically not the same thing as East London. Outsiders might mix up the two terms, but no Guermantes ever distinguished himself more jealously from a Courvoisier than a true East Ender did from an East Londoner. But what exactly was the true East End? Here there was ample room for disagreement. One of the best books ever written about the area, by Millicent Rose, extends the definition to include Poplar (which seems to me not quite right) and Hackney (which seems to me quite wrong). At the other extreme, Thomas Burke, well known in his day as a romantic chronicler of the East End, confined himself firmly to Stepney. This seems to me too narrow: I think any reasonable definition has to take in Bethnal Green as well. But I would like to have been able to agree with Burke. 'Our' East End, that of my family and friends, was certainly Stepney; Bethnal Green seemed rough and menacing in comparison, not least because it was known to have been a stronghold of Mosleyites before the war.

Even within Stepney itself, there were many subdivisions. The more important of them were marked on the map – Aldgate, Spitalfields, Whitechapel, Stepney Green, Mile End, Bow (along with Wapping and the adjacent riverside areas, which formed yet another world on its own). But there were finer gradations as well, mini-neighbourhoods created by building developments and street plans, by the presence of a landmark or the preponderance of a trade.

Some of these small areas were themselves rich in variety. Black Lion Yard, for instance, was a cobbled alley running between Whitechapel Road and Old Montague Street. From the main road you hardly noticed it; when you turned into it, however, you found that it was a kind of Hatton Garden of the East, lined with jewellers' shops on both sides. And for good measure, amid the windows full of watches and rings, there was a disused wooden gate, just beginning to rot, with the legend 'Evans and Son – Cowkeepers' painted on it in both English and Yiddish characters, and underneath (also in English and Yiddish) the slogan 'Fresh from the Cow'.

But when I think of Black Lion Yard, it isn't only the Yard itself I recall. Just along from it, there was an odd little hiccup in Whitechapel Road, where the pavement widened and a couple of well-known shops stood at right angles to the road – Mazin's, a leading Jewish bookseller, and the hairdressing establishment of Professor Adolph Cohen (under whose tutelage a number of celebrated West End hairdressers, including Vidal Sassoon, got their start). And then across the road there was the famous Whitechapel Bell Foundry, with a continuous history dating back to Elizabethan times. And near the foundry there was the pavement exchange, with tailors milling around looking for work and noticeboards advertising vacancies for button-hole makers and Hoffman pressers. The foundry, happily, is still there. Everything else, for better or worse, has gone; Black Lion Yard has been wiped off the map and replaced by a shiny office block called Black Lion House.

History, in various shapes, lay all around. Near the beginning of Mile End Road, just past the big Whitechapel breweries, stood the Trinity Almshouses. I didn't really know anything about them, but I could see that they were old and handsome and I had heard that they had a connection with Trinity House and the sea: that at least was something. I was impressed, too, when my father told me that *he* had heard that a house across the way had been the home of Captain Cook. But what appealed to me even more – a historical legacy of another kind – was the combination, you might almost say the comedy team, of Wickham and Spiegelhalter. Wickham's, next door to the almshouses, was a department store (of Edwardian vintage, I imagine), with an imposing colonnaded façade which wouldn't have looked out of place in Regent Street. In buying the land for the site, however, the owners had failed to dislodge a small jewellery shop called Spiegelhalter. They had gone ahead none the less, Spiegelhalter had stood his ground, and the result was that the façade suddenly gave way to a modest two-storey frontage ('Spiegelhalter the East End Jewellers') and then resumed its majestic sweep. The effect was rather like that of a row of Grenadier Guards standing to attention, with a little old man where one of them ought to have been. I rejoiced in Spiegelhalter's stubbornness. I also assumed (not unreasonably, given his name, the neighbourhood and the nature of his business) that he was Jewish, a *kleine menshele* who had decided to dig his heels in. But you never can tell. Years later, I discovered that the Spiegelhalters – they had had the business for generations – were German Lutherans.

A good deal of East End lore lingered on from pre-war days. I was strongly aware of the old Labour leader George Lansbury, for instance, even though he had resigned as leader in the year I had been born and died in 1940. This is largely because he had lived and worked at our end of town. He had been MP for the next-door constituency, Bow; he was famous for having gone to prison when he was on Poplar council rather than authorise payments to the LCC which he said the impoverished borough couldn't afford. My mother's father, it will be recalled, had been a subscriber to his paper, *Lansbury's Labour Weekly*. My mother sometimes saw him walking along Bow Road when she took me out in my pram.

Within the Jewish community, some of the leading personalities of the immigrant period were still household names. Some of them, indeed, were still alive and active. There was J.K. Goldbloom, headmaster of a Talmud Torah in Stepney for fifty years and pioneer of the 'Hebrew in Hebrew' teaching method (a kindred spirit, here at least, of Rouse of the Perse). At a much more prominent level, there was the mathematician and Zionist leader Selig Brodetsky. Brodetsky's achievement in being elected senior wrangler at Cambridge before the First World War had echoed round the community, and reverberated long afterwards. He was a true child of the ghetto – foreign-born, the son of a *shammes*. His success, altogether exceptional though it was at the time, held out hope for those who came after him.

If the history of the East End caught my imagination, so did its hustle and bustle and its sights and sounds. Who, with the slightest feeling for the human comedy, could fail to take pleasure in the tailor in Wentworth Street who had changed his name – if his signboard was to be believed – to 'Abe Wentworth', or the cinema in Brick Lane which chose to call itself the Mayfair, or the curious, often Yiddish-derived turns of phrase which you heard in East End conversations ('the wedding was a lovely affair and, you should excuse me, we had cocktails')? Who could fail to respond to the sight of the old woman swathed in overalls, sitting at the street corner selling bagels, or the poultry market in Hessel Street, or the flow of life along Whitechapel Road?* There were quiet streets and dull stretches in the East End; but there were also scenes with the animation of a boulevard or a bazaar.

All this may sound rather like the talk of a tourist, however – and with some reason. For the truth is that any claim I had to be an East Ender had to be severely qualified. I was a resident rather than a native. My middle-class background, the schools I went to, and the decisive difference which Egham had made all set me apart. I was sheltered from the rougher aspects of East End

---

* The word 'bagel', I should add, had been cockneyfied in the East End and was pronounced 'beigel', with a long *i*-sound. Anyone asking for a bagel would have been regarded as very refained.

existence; I knew that once I had grown up I would be free to leave whenever I wanted to. That isn't to say that my physical surroundings didn't make a difference, or that there weren't plenty of casual social contacts. Today, when I fall into conversation with an old East Ender – a taxi driver, as often as not – we usually find enough common ground for us to share a joke or pool a little nostalgia. But it is all fairly superficial. To read an account of an authentic, unmitigated East End childhood – a detailed account, such as you find in William Goldman's *East End My Cradle*, or Emanuel Litvinoff's *Journey Through a Small Planet*, or Steven Berkoff's *Free Association* – is a more disconcerting experience. There is common ground, but there is also a great gulf. They describe a world I knew about, but which I didn't know.

Naturally, I felt more at home in our immediate neighbourhood. Not with our next-door neighbours on one side – a father who flew into mad rages, a large family who fought back. (There were shouting matches which shook the rafters.) But on the other side there were neighbours who were good company – Lou, who worked for a furrier, and his brother Harry, who was something in the rag trade, and their sister Debbie, and their brother-in-law Dave, a tailor who looked as if he needed a good night's sleep but was always being dragged off by Debbie to the latest film or (in the fullness of time, when cappuccinos came in) the latest Soho coffee bar. The family had had a difficult start in life, but they were anything but downtrodden. Both brothers were good-looking and smartly turned out – Lou had a 1930s film star moustache – and full of cheerful wisecracks. One of the things which made them seem bright and up-to-date in my eyes is that they were avid readers of *Time* magazine, which they used to pass on to me.

The Mile End area was a mixed one. Our most likeable neighbour was a sturdy open-faced Cornishman called Oates, not long arrived in London. Round the corner an ancient couple called Green ran a tiny grocer's shop, very much old East End, with barrels (none of them magic, alas) full of herrings and pickles. The local stretch of the Mile End Road was spacious and tree-lined. There were mean streets nearby, and pleasant ones. There were two decent grammar schools in the immediate neighbourhood, and a building which had once been a workhouse, and, even more forbidding, the sealed-off world of St Clement's mental hospital; there was Spratts' dog-biscuit factory, with a large sign attached to it which always fascinated me as a child – the word 'Spratts' shaped to form the outline of a terrier. In retrospect, though no one could have foreseen it at the time, the square into which we moved after the war, Tredegar Square, was an obvious candidate for the gentrification which it eventually received, long after we had gone: one side of it in particular looked like a discarded chunk of Belgravia. The next street, Coborn Road, had the distinction of having provided the music-hall singer Charles Coborn, *né* McCallum, with his stage name. (Coborn, whose career went back to the 1870s, had died as recently as 1945. His most famous songs were 'Two Lovely Black Eyes' and 'The Man Who Broke the Bank at Monte Carlo'.)

I went out a few times with local boys, but there was too much awkwardness for any kind of lasting friendship to develop. And they were, so to speak, from the respectable end of the market, grammar school boys hoping to end up in one of the professions. Beyond lay a world of jukeboxes and dance halls which I only glimpsed, beyond that the real tearaways.

Crime was meant to be a great East End tradition. There was certainly plenty of it: my father had a number of patients who were habitual small-time offenders, families who usually had at least one member 'inside'. But the notion that the average East Ender of those days lived a life shadowed by crime seems to me nonsense. Neighbours trusted one another; the streets, if you used a little common sense, were safe – or as safe as streets in a poor part of a big city are ever likely to be.

At the same time the idea of crime was undoubtedly invested with a certain glamour. I felt it myself, hearing about East End spielers or gambling clubs, reading stories about East End gangs and villains. I got a buzz seeing some of the flashier types who hung around the Mile End Arena, and a bigger buzz when the Arena featured briefly in *It Always Rains on Sunday* (the only film I have seen which captures the genuine feel of the East End of the period). But all this was a fantasy game, far removed from the world where people actually got hurt. I knew almost nothing of what was really going on. I was twenty before I first heard the name of the most celebrated villain to emerge from the East End before the Krays, Jack Comer alias Jack Spot.

That was in 1955, when everyone learned his name, after his knife-fight in broad daylight in Soho – 'the Battle of Frith Street'. The affair and its aftermath filled the papers for weeks, and I followed them with passionate interest. Some of the details were indeed extraordinary, such as the Ealing comedies subplot, involving the eighty-eight-year-old Anglican clergyman, in hock to the bookmakers, who had supplied perjured evidence. But what gave the whole story its particular spice, even though it all took place 'up west', was Jack Spot's East End background. I knew, or thought I knew, where he was coming from; and it was an undoubted point in his favour that he had the reputation of having fought the fascists, and inflicted damage on them, in the 1930s. If the hard men played by Cagney or Edward G. Robinson in the movies had their allure, why not Jack Spot?

A few years ago he was interviewed on television, and it is a measure of how far I had been tempted to mix up gangster myth with gangster reality that I should have been surprised by what an unpleasant impression he made. Recalling some of his exploits with a razor, he was downright revolting, and only once did he strike the note I'd been hoping for – when he described his old rival Billy Hill, whom he had long outlived, as 'the richest man in the cemetery'.

For a time I was equally intrigued by another rogue, though one of a very different stamp – and in his case, if only for an instant, our paths crossed. One of the big stories of the winter of 1948 was the Lynskey Tribunal, an inquiry into allegations of ministerial corruption. The sums involved were relatively small: what gave the affair its popular appeal was the personality of the central figure, a 'contact man' or fixer living in Park Lane called Sidney Stanley. His apparent affability, his chutzpah, his evasive answers and his general bogusness made excellent copy. His pasty features and heavy-lidded eyes gazed out from many a front page – and the first time my father saw a picture of him in the *Evening Standard*, he exclaimed, 'It's Rechtand!' Schlomo Rechtand, that is, someone he had known in his early days in Whitechapel. I wondered whether he had made a mistake; but sure enough, as the tribunal progressed it was revealed that one of the names Stanley had used (he had had a number) was 'Stanley Rechtand'. Later that year there was further confirmation, not that any was needed. We were on holiday in Paris, walking down an avenue near the Gare de l'Est, when a figure wearing a belted overcoat approached from the other direction. This time *I* had no difficulty in recognising who it was, from photographs. My father greeted him (as Rechtand), and introduced us; they chatted for a couple of minutes. I don't think Stanley was particularly pleased by the encounter, and we parted without much of a farewell. But I felt as though I had brushed against the hem of true Notoriety.

There is a postscript. A dozen years later I contributed a chapter on the Lynskey Tribunal to a book about the post-war era edited by Philip French and Michael Sissons, *The Age of Austerity*. It was my first appearance between hard covers, and the first review which mentioned my contribution was by Clement Attlee, no less. He confined himself to observing, in the driest of tones, that he didn't think the subject was worth writing about. I consoled myself with the thought that the comment was at any rate thoroughly Attlee-esque.

Most East End Jews, the bad boys and wide boys notwithstanding, were thoroughly respectable. Not prissy or genteel, though a few of them were that too, but hard-working, law-abiding, imbued with family values, observant of the social decencies. I think the same was true of most of their non-Jewish neighbours, but I confine myself to what I know best. And Jews had an additional inducement to respectability. The world harboured some large prejudices against them. It was dinned into Jewish children that they were liable to be judged by the worst among them rather than the best, and that if they got into trouble they would be bringing shame on the community as well as themselves.

Of course, the rougher side of life was never far away. Nowadays, when a fashionable play showers the audience with four-letter words, or an acclaimed novel drags its readers through the mud, I am tempted to murmur, what's new? These are things whose existence everyone in the East End fifty years ago took for granted. It is just that nobody thought they belonged in a book or on the stage.

To try to sum up such an area in a few phrases would be absurd: there was far too much variety. But there *were* representative types – and one collective face which I see when I think of the East End is a face lined with experience, unillusioned, a little grumpy, limited but shrewd, not too refined but not too coarse either. It is the same kind of face that I picture when I read some favourite lines of mine (they are about New York, but they would do just as well for London) by the American light-versifier Samuel Hoffenstein:

> I'm fond of doctors and drivers of hacks
> Whose names are Morris and Barney and Max;
> I'm fond of waiters in places I know
> Whose names are Louis and Mike and Joe . . .

Let me not be too sentimental. I have met some very boring Barneys and some very boorish Mikes. But I think that the hard-wearing virtues which Hoffenstein's poem conjures up (without having to name them) were real enough.

One characteristic of the Jewish East End which may not have been universal, but which was very strongly marked, was ambition. Few people were so fond of the area that they didn't want to get out of it. Most East Enders were anxious to move up and move on: the great escape route was business, and the business of the area was above all the clothing trade. No one who lived there could have failed to be aware of its significance, or of the streetsmart mentality which supposedly went with it – 'I can get it for you wholesale' – or of the large sums of money which it yielded, often in cramped quarters: there was a joke about a Rolls-Royce which was seen manoeuvring its way down an alley in Whitechapel, bearing plates which read 'CD' and 'GB' – 'coats and dresses, gowns and blouses'. Jews were well represented in other trades, too, and the really big money lay elsewhere, in property and retailing, but for the East End at that time the archetypal *alrightnik* was still the successful garment manufacturer.

The old sweatshop conditions were by now no more than a memory, but the buildings of that era, where they had been spared by the bombs, still stood all around. My father had a patient, with whom he was on gruff good terms, called Schaffer – 'Schaffer the trouser-maker'. One day he was summoned to Schaffer's work-shop (someone had been taken ill). I went along in the car, and when we got there, he suggested that I go in with him; when I held back, he said, 'If you want to be a writer, you ought to see how people live.' After that I felt I had no choice, so I followed him into the workshop – a long low building, rather like a converted stable. The two things which impressed me most were the scraps of waste material lying on the floor near the machines – they were known as 'cabbage' – and the fact that most of the workmen seemed to be in their fifties or sixties. (What I didn't realise at the time was that young people were deserting the trade for more attractive jobs, and that the traditional Jewish tailoring worker was already on the way out.)

Years later, I was having dinner with an American professor and his wife in a restaurant off Leicester Square, and there at a nearby table, looking very natty, was Schaffer the trouser-maker. I was surprised that he recognised me, but he waved his fingers in a token salute. 'Why,' said the professor, 'it's just like New York.' I felt quite proud.

My parents deplored the worship of money, and they had many reservations about businessmen as a class. My father had seen some of his patients and his acquaintances grow rich, and he didn't think that they were necessarily wiser or kinder than the ones they had left behind. My mother had been particularly put out by an advertisement she had once come across announcing a vacancy for an 'aggressive' salesman. It summed up all her misgivings about a world in which she was glad to have no part.

On the whole I absorbed these values, but my inward attitude was more complicated. I had no thought of going into business myself (or into any business except the business of literature). If I had been misguided enough to embark on a commercial career, I don't suppose I would have lasted a week. But at some point I became fascinated with the idea of wealth – the idea rather than the reality, and not so much the acquisitions of great men as the manner in which they had been acquired. One thing which started me off was a radio programme about Sir Thomas Lipton. (He seems a very dim hero now.) Then, partly because our local branch of the library was particularly well stocked with American books, I moved on to robber barons and transatlantic tycoons. I was gripped by Frederick Lewis Allen's *The Great Pierpont Morgan*, and by a popular novel based on the Duponts called *Dynasty of Death*. At the cinema, I thrilled to the sonorities of the *March of Time* pastiche at the beginning of *Citizen Kane*. ('Last week, as it must to all men, death came to Charles Foster Kane.') And when I began reading the novels of Theodore Dreiser, the one which impressed me most, though it is not his best, was *The Financier*, the first part of his trilogy about the career of a nineteenth-century magnate called Frank Cowperwood. I was half-fascinated, half-repelled by the allegory of the struggle for existence in the opening chapter, in which a lobster slowly devours a squid. (This was a bad lobster, infinitely worse than a mere *lobbes*.) But what really drew me in was the episode soon afterwards in which the young Cowperwood's banker-father fires his imagination – the date is around 1850 – by showing him a rarity, an East India Company share certificate which a client has left with him as collateral for a loan. The scene overlapped in my mind with a childhood memory of my own father holding up a crisp five-pound note, of the old, black-and-white, beautifully engraved variety, and telling me, 'Have a look, you won't often see one of these.' (A five-pound note – ah, inflation.)

If ambition was in the air, there were times when the atmosphere seemed charged with something related, perhaps, but vaguer and more dramatic. I can only call it, portentous though it may sound, the sense that one had a destiny. The street lights coming on at dusk, a looming sky, the long perspectives of the main road could all induce a sudden recognition (as though for the first time) that unknown circumstances lay ahead, that faces and voices one couldn't guess at lay in wait. It was a turbulent sensation, far removed from the simple exhilaration of 'The God of Fair Beginnings'; it had a counterpart in the feelings stirred by some of the more doomy titles of novels that caught my eye in the library – *The Mortal Storm*, *Nobody Lives For Ever*, *London Belongs to Me*. But while it lasted, it made life seem far more intense.

Moods of this kind were at their strongest in my early teens.

They obviously reflected the uncertainties of adolescence, sexual and otherwise; and if I associated them with the East End more than anywhere else, it was largely because that was where I happened to find myself most of the time. Other sights and scenes prompted them, too. Yet I still feel that they were especially appropriate to the area – marked as it was by restlessness and fractured traditions; heavily populated as it had been by immigrants, and as it still was by the children of immigrants, by people who seldom expected (or wanted) to see their lives end on the streets where they had begun.

Not that exalted moods were liable to last long in the East End: there was too much about the place calculated to bring one down to earth. An accumulation of poverty, for one thing. Rusty pipes, mottled paintwork, mildew, sour smells; bomb damage which revealed quite how meagre the interiors of many of the houses had been. But there was also abundant energy, and a constant appetite for amusement and entertainment. For sport, especially. Limited though my own interest in it was, few names bring back the period as sharply as those of such urban heroes as Split Waterman the speedway rider and Bert Assirati the all-in wrestler. Someone who made even more of an impression was Jack Solomons, the fishmonger-turned-boxing promoter who seemed to stage all the big fights: I accorded him a high place in my private pantheon. And though the great days of East End Jewish boxing, of Kid Lewis and Kid Berg, were long since gone, a few Jewish fighters could still be seen in the ring. The best-known of them was Al Phillips, 'the Aldgate Tiger'. There were also two brothers, Lew and Harry Lazar. Harry was my grandmother's lodger for a time.

Among the posters which plastered the walls, for sporting events, dances and the rest, the ones which intrigued me most were those for the Queen's Theatre, Poplar. The only surviving music hall in the area, it had never been a major house, and now it was drifting into a twilight zone in which Olde Tyme compilations and variety were interspersed with striptease: one show which turned up there was called *Yes! We Have No Pyjamas*, another was called *Nudes of the World*. I knew that at thirteen or fourteen there was no chance of my being allowed to see them, and it was equally clear that within a few years traditional music hall would be

extinct. As though to compensate, I became a music-hall enthusi-
ast in the abstract. With little to go on beyond the occasional BBC
broadcast, I read everything about the halls I could find in the
library, and I developed an affection – almost as though I had
actually seen them – not only for the obvious great names, but for
lesser luminaries as well; for such figures as Gus Elen, Harry
Champion, Ella Shields and Florrie Forde.

Ella Shields was someone whom in principle I *could* have seen.
She was still going strong in the late 1940s, and I recall her name
heading the list of attractions on a Queen's Theatre poster. Her
most famous number, about a tramp mimicking a man about
town, was 'Burlington Bertie from Bow' – and as Bow was just
down the road from Mile End this gave her the added appeal of
being an honorary local girl. But then the supreme music-hall
artist, Marie Lloyd, had been a genuine local product (or almost
local – she grew up in Hoxton). And lots of music-hall songs
evoked a world which, to anyone living in Stepney, seemed very
close at hand – Gus Elen's 'If It Wasn't for the 'Ouses in Between',
for instance, with its mournful account of his hemmed-in little
patch of a back garden ('With a ladder and some glasses/You
could see to 'Ackney Marshes . . .'). The music hall took the whole
country for its constituency, and it spoke for ordinary people
everywhere. But nowhere was its spirit stronger than in East
London.

There was another form of theatre-going that I missed out on –
to my subsequent regret, though I was only fitfully aware of it at
the time. The Yiddish theatre had once played an important part
in the life of the East End. Its earlier history, or what I have read of
it, had been colourful and enterprising: I would love to have been
present at the Yiddish production of *Rigoletto* in 1912, or the
Yiddish production of Strindberg's *The Father* the previous year
(at a time when the play had not yet been produced in English). By
the post-1945 period, however, the audience for Yiddish plays of
any kind had inevitably dwindled. The best-known Yiddish
theatre in London, the Pavilion in Whitechapel Road, had closed
its doors back in the thirties, and subsequently been bombed: for a
long time after the war its shell still stood, a fantastic wreck, with

what had once been the auditorium open to the sky. (When I peeked inside, there were ferns growing out of the plush.)

Yet theatrical life persisted. There were Yiddish seasons at the big Alexandra Theatre in Stoke Newington, and for a time, all the talk among my grandmother and her friends was of a hit musical there called *Der Galitzianer Koboy* ('The Cowboy from Galicia' – Galicia in Eastern Europe, needless to say, not the one in Spain). And, much more remarkably, a full-time Yiddish theatre kept going in the East End until 1970 – the Grand Palais in Commercial Road.

My parents' visits to the Grand Palais, though they didn't go there very often, meant a lot to them. The question of taking me with them never came up: I would have been unable to follow most of what was going on. I don't even know what plays they saw, although I'm fairly sure that one of them was an old Yiddish favourite, *Di Rumenishe Chasene* ('The Romanian Wedding'). But they sometimes talked about the actors – Meyer Tselniker, Jenny Lovitch, Millie Chissick and a few others – and I heard enough to realise that the productions were marked by an exceptional rapport between performers and audience. They were the occasion for shared jokes, shared emotions, revived memories and the instant recognition of character traits and social types, with the artistic quality of what was being staged no more than a secondary consideration. The time came when I wished that I had taken a look for myself; but by then the Grand Palais had been turned into a bingo hall, and it was too late.

There was a third theatre, only a single stop away on the Tube, which I went to once or twice – the Theatre Royal, Stratford East, run in those days by an actor called David Horne. The plays he put on were standard repertory fare, and it was a pleasant enough place, but it didn't seem to have much connection with the life going on all around it. For that one had to wait until Joan Littlewood took over, with electrifying effect, a few years later.

Plays were also on offer closer to home, at the People's Palace in Mile End Road. The original People's Palace, opened by Queen Victoria in the year of her Golden Jubilee, had been designed, in a patronising spirit, to bring Culture to the masses, and the modern building which had replaced it was adorned with a frieze bearing witness to the same ideal. There was a graceful figure holding up a copy of Ruskin's *Unto This Last*, for instance. But the scheme hadn't worked in Victorian times, and it wasn't working now: few of the shows that were put on aspired to be anything more than middlebrow entertainment. That didn't stop me enjoying some of them, the antiquated musical comedies in particular. (Where else would I have had a chance to catch up with *The Quaker Girl*?) But I don't think they were the kind of thing Ruskin would have approved of. The People's Palace finally gave up the fight in the 1950s; the building was taken over by Queen Mary College, its next-door neighbour.

A cultural implant in the East End which worked far more successfully (partly, perhaps, because it didn't depend as much on local patronage) was the Whitechapel Art Gallery. Of the exhibitions which I saw there, one had an especially strong impact: a show commemorating Mark Gertler, who had died ten years previously. What set it apart were the pictures in which Gertler drew on his early life in Whitechapel – the portraits of his mother, the melancholy *Jewish Family*, the more modernistic and metallic *Rabbi and Rabbitzin*. Even at fourteen, my age at the time, I would have argued against the idea that art had a duty to serve ethnic or communal ends. It was a philistine heresy. But that didn't mean that artistic inspiration and ethnic or communal feeling couldn't sometimes intersect, as they did here. I felt curiously liberated. The pictures were not only touching; they were proof that the world I knew was as available for art as anywhere else.

Images and incidents are easier to recall than states of mind. The emotions of one period become overlaid by those of another, and in trying to recollect what I felt about the East End while I was growing up, I realise that my memories may well have been coloured, and softened, by memories of what I felt when I looked back at some later date. It is possible that at the time I resented the disadvantages of living there more than I am willing to admit.

One thing I know for certain, however, is that I had no sense of being trapped. The chief effect of any dissatisfaction I felt was simply to sharpen my appetite for other parts of London, for the city at large.

11

Big City

An extraordinary city, London. A wonderful city – or so I felt. Not every hour of every day. It could seem heavy and dreary, too, and much of the time, I had no feelings about it either way. But when I did think about it, my imagination, for the most part, came alive. Scenes composed themselves into townscapes, buildings seemed steeped in atmosphere.

If the very name London, at such times, suggested a picture book, the city also lay open like a storybook. As you looked around, its dramatic potential seemed endless. It was fascinating to glance at a window or a door, and to dwell on possibilities – on the lives that might once have been lived behind them, and the lives that were still being lived; on plans that had been pondered, liaisons, quarrels, secret histories, deals that were about to be clinched.

To add to the drama, there were constant reminders of the war. The most obvious were the bomb sites, with willowherb growing out of the rubble, low walls to stop you falling into what had once been basements, clumps of prefabs – boxes for living in – where real houses had once stood. 'Britain Can Take It', the wartime slogan had said. Britain *had* taken it. And though I don't recall hearing much open exultation (the mood was convalescent rather than triumphant), there was an unmistakable low-key pride. It was what helped to underwrite the belief that London was still the greatest city in the world. That, and the sheer weight of the past.

Time shifts our perspectives. To a boy growing up in the late 1940s, the Victorian era seemed utterly remote. We were living, after all, in the Atomic Age; layer after layer of history had intervened. Fifty years on, however, the gap doesn't seem quite so wide. I remember being enthralled by the trailer for a film version of *An Ideal Husband* – this was in 1947 or 1948 – with the commentator's voice promising that I would be transported back to a fabulous world 'where the women were wasp-waisted and the men were wasp-witted'. It is disconcerting to reflect that today, in the year 2000, we are further away from the film than the film was from the first night of Wilde's play. But then in retrospect whole aspects of the England of the 1940s seem far more Victorian, or quasi-Victorian, than they did at the time. It was a country where the front page of *The Times* carried nothing but classified advertisements; where audiences stood to attention for the national anthem (even in Mile End); where the only summer break many of my father's patients had was when they went 'hopping' in Kent; where judges put on the black cap before sentencing men to death.

Nowhere were the appointed roles and rituals more strongly marked than in London. Stockjobbers, market porters, rag-and-bone men all dressed for the part. Institutions and traditions were firmly in place, sustained by a degree of confidence which has long since been lost. The rules were there to be kept.

At the same time, as though by contrast, the city rejoiced in its anomalies and eccentricities. Newspapers ran daily reports on the minor humours of magistrates' courts. Local quirks were cherished. And the prevailing formality meant that exotic blooms stood out all the more brightly. I can recall how excited I was when I saw the famous black racing tipster Prince Monolulu walking along in Hyde Park. (He was wearing his ostrich plumes, although apparently off duty: I can't claim that I heard him shout, as he used to, 'I gotta horse.') No doubt he would still turn heads today; but in a world which has been saturated with 'outrageous' celebrities, he could hardly seem as much of a nonpareil as he did then.

Although everyone knew that London was a vast sprawl, there was also a strong urge to think of it as homely and compact. 'London Town' was a potent phrase. It was largely a myth, of course – the myth of the Lord Mayor's golden coach, as oppposed to the great grey reality (at that time) of the London County Council. I had an aunt – only a few years older than I was, so more like a big sister – who used to chant a playground rhyme:

> I am a Girl Guide dressed in blue,
> And these are the things that I must do.
> Salute to the King, bow to the Queen,
> And fall right down to the LCC.

The LCC was where the power lay. But myths have their own power, and indeed their own reality. You couldn't bring yourself to care much who the Leader of the LCC was. The Lord Mayor, on the other hand, was the direct heir of Dick Whittington.

One thing I regretted, the other side of the coin, was that London didn't seem very good at Modernity. It was a game at which New York had beaten us, and by the look of it always would. There were some buildings which seemed to me satisfyingly streamlined – Shell-Mex House, seen from the Embankment; Broadcasting House; the Dorchester; Battersea Power Station. (I was impressed, the first time I heard it, when a teacher described power stations as 'the cathedrals of the twentieth century'.) But even as a boy I shuddered away from the Stalinoid hulk of Senate House, and I could see, in an untutored way, that most of the new flats and office blocks rising up were mediocre. No, what London did best was the past.

My mother used to speak affectionately about what she called 'old London', by which she meant anything that was both old and good (a fine terrace, a decent church) without being an obvious landmark. My father, though architecture didn't mean much to him, took satisfaction in the thought that London was dotted with curious survivals – the Cheshire Cheese, the pseudo-Roman baths in the Strand. Between them, they must have predisposed me to take an interest in 'old London' myself, although I think it would have seduced me anyway. My enthusiasm was impressionistic and unsystematic. Later on, I found a good deal of what I would have liked to say expressed in such essays in appreciation as James Bone's *The London Perambulator* and V.S. Pritchett's *London Perceived*. (If you want to sample Bone's skill at evoking a quarter, try his chapter on the dingy region he describes as 'North o' Euston'.) I didn't read such books until I was an adult; but the appetite for them had been formed while I was a child.

Increasingly, as I grew up, my responses to London became coloured by literature at large. Sometimes – though on the whole these were the least evocative – the associations were directly biographical: Dickens had lived at this address, Thackeray had worked at that one. Sometimes, when a location in a story or a poem was unspecified, I would find myself thinking of an actual site which fitted the bill. And sometimes a literary reference was completely vague, and endlessly suggestive. When I was fourteen or fifteen, for instance, I saw a ballet in Paris based on Apollinaire's poem *Le Chanson du Mal-aimé*. The ballet didn't make much of an impression, but the poem did: it is the one that opens, 'Un soir de demi-brume à Londres', and goes on to describe the poet's encounter with 'a ruffian who resembled my love', and the surreal journey which followed. The London of the poem is a dream-London, and one that in any case is soon left behind; but the phrase 'un soir de demi-brume à Londres' reverberated, and cast its spell over the real London.

Generally, however, it was the references to specific places, places I knew, which registered most. A street or a district only had to be mentioned in a book for it to acquire additional interest, you might almost say additional depth. In Joseph Conrad's *Victory*, for instance, the forlorn young musician Lena recalls her disrupted childhood in lodgings off Kingsland Road. I had been down Kingsland Road many times, but after I had read *Victory* I saw it through new eyes – Lena's eyes, Conrad's eyes. It was more fully human. And though Bernard Shaw isn't usually the man to go to for atmosphere, he conferred some on the streets north of Victoria Park by situating the Reverend James Morrell's parsonage on one of them in *Candida*. They, too, were streets I knew, in the sense of having seen them or driven through them; but it took *Candida* to rescue them from anonymity.

One of the entries in James Morrell's diary is for a meeting of the 'Social-Democratic Federation, Mile End branch'. Victoria Park lies immediately to the north of Mile End, Kingsland Road a mile or two to the north-east. They were both points of entry for what we used to call 'North London'. In fact it was no more than a slice of north-east London, stopping well short of the suburbs. It isn't all that big if you look at it on the map. But it seemed vast enough as we criss-crossed it on family visits and expeditions. It took me a long time to get the hang of the exact geographical relationship between Dalston and Clapton, Hackney Downs and Stamford Hill, Stoke Newington and Amhurst Park. I'm not sure that I have got it even now.

'North London' marked the commonest first stage in the Jewish move away from the East End. After that came the sunny uplands of 'North-West London', which meant primarily Golders Green, Hendon and the suburbs beyond. (It was where almost all my Jewish classmates at the City of London lived.) There were variations, but the main lines of dispersal were firmly laid down. I recall a story – apocryphal, no doubt – about a wedding reception in Stamford Hill. A local boy was marrying a girl from Hendon, and one of the guests was supposed to have said to her, 'Young lady, what are you doing here? You're going backwards.'

With both my grandmothers living in the area and with a thick sprinkling of uncles, aunts and cousins, north London inevitably became the part of London, outside the East End, which I knew best. Occasionally, too, my father would visit a friend in Stoke Newington or Stamford Hill of the type he could no longer find locally. There was one snowy-haired businessman-scholar whose library had accumulated to the point where books were stacked all over the floor, with narrow passageways left between them.

Yet despite these links I was less taken with 'North London' than with many other parts of the city. One reason, probably the principal one, is that I increasingly associated our visits there with family tensions and acerbities – not between my parents, but involving them; all about nothing, in that the issues they turned on were slight, but all about everything, in that they were fuelled by long-pent-up jealousies. My father, poor man, found it hard to cope with these troubles. My mother's reaction was simply to freeze – my own reaction, too, though compounded in my case with deep embarrassment. I hated scenes. I longed to distance myself from what I privately thought of (I don't know where I had picked up the phrase) as 'Jewish emotionalism'.

These inflamed episodes were only part of the story. Most of our family visits remained friendly, or at worst routine. And I have many pleasant memories of north London excursions – to Springfield Park, for example, watching the old men chinwagging away on the park benches. (Having once overheard a group of them arguing about politics, we jokily assumed that that was what they were always talking about, and nicknamed them 'the Parliament'). Still, something about the area eluded me. It was too amorphous; a diluted, more prosperous East End, yet curiously unlike it, too; in many ways, as far as I was concerned, more daunting.

Around 1980, not long after we first met, the difference between Hackney and the East End came up in a conversation I had with Harold Pinter. (Harold had often been described in the press, quite inaccurately, as an 'East End dramatist'.) Antonia Fraser suggested that we go on an expedition to see the street where he had grown up, in Hackney – which we did, a few weeks later. As we drove out, Harold remarked that it saved time to tell people he came from Hackney, because everyone had heard of it, but that in fact he thought of himself as coming from a part of Hackney called Clapton. No problem there; *I'd* certainly heard of Clapton. Then, as we drove on, it was as though we were going deeper and deeper into a dream, until we finally pulled up in Thistlewaite Road – the street where my grandmother (my father's mother) had lived, along with an uncle and aunt and their children. Harold had lived opposite; he remembered them well and spoke of them quite warmly.

I hadn't been back to Thistlewaite Road for twenty-five years, and all kinds of memories came tumbling into my mind. I thought of how my uncle had died suddenly, in early middle age, and of the pathos of the fact that he had just had a new suit made. I thought of Lea Bridge Road, which begins round the corner, and of how when I was small it had seemed to me the longest road in the world. But I also thought about the early plays of Harold Pinter. So this, in a manner of speaking, was where they had their origin.

I was reminded of that day a few years later, while talking to Zvi Jagendorf, a friend who taught at the Hebrew University in Jerusalem, but who had spent his childhood in Clapton. He told me that the first time he saw *The Birthday Party* and *The Homecoming* he came out of the theatre saying to himself: 'Clapton! That's the way people talk in Clapton and Stoke Newington and Dalston.' And though I'm not enough of a Henry Higgins to work out why, I know what he meant. It isn't a question of social realism, I need hardly say, or even of verbal realism. Everything has been heightened, distorted, rendered more mysterious. But when all due qualifications have been made, there still seems to me an unmistakable local touch about early Pinter. North London – one aspect of north London – has found its commemoration.

Like many Londoners born north of the river, I grew up knowing very little of south London; much of it might have been as remote as the south bank of the Amazon. My thoughts didn't often stray eastwards, either. But the west beckoned, as it says in one of Auden's poems, like a wicked uncle.

From early on, I was fascinated by the idea of the West End. I dreamed of exploring it, of entering into its excitements, of mastering its intricacies. That there were different West Ends packed together, so near and yet so far – that Burlington House, say, was only a short walk from Brewer Street – was all part of the appeal. I relished the juxtapositions, and the variety. But if there was one West End quality which seemed to me supreme it was Sophistication, which I chiefly located in the upper reaches of show business.

Noël Coward was a key figure in this respect, on account of his songs rather than his plays (which I hadn't yet seen), and still more on account of his sleek public persona. My brother was now old enough to share some of my enthusiasms, and we used to play a record of Coward singing Coward again and again – almost as often as we played our records of Danny Kaye. (Our particular favourite was 'The Stately Homes of England'.) But then the whole Coward act worked for me, dressing gowns, clipped accent and all. I remember the pleasure I got from a competition in a magazine, in which competitors had to devise famous last words for people who were still alive, and the winning entry for Coward was 'I think He'll be too, too divine'.

It was much easier to go to the local library than to get to a West End theatre and, as with the music hall, my appetite for Sophistication was initially fed largely with books. I became something of a precocious antiquarian: along with biographies of Wilde and other mainstream figures, I cheerfully immersed myself in memoirs with such titles as *I Remember Romano's*. (Romano's had been a famous restaurant in the Strand.) As a result, my image of the West End was in many ways lushly Edwardian or floridly Late Victorian. But I was even more interested in the twenties and thirties: what epoch more intriguing than the one just before one was born? And among the lesser figures of that period there was one in particular who haunted me, partly because it was so difficult to find out anything about him. John Tilley, who died in 1935, had been my father's favourite comedian. That alone would have been enough to confer mythic status on him. But the mythic became the positively mystical as I gradually discovered how forgotten he was – and still is. He seems to have dropped out of the memoirs and histories of entertainment almost completely.*

Meanwhile, real theatres were still staging real shows, and mere book-knowledge wasn't going to satisfy me for long. My quest for Sophistication became focused on intimate revues. I had read about them in the papers, and heard about them on the BBC, and I nagged my parents until they took me to one, a show called *Sauce Tartare*. On the whole I found it as entertaining and generally enchanting as I had hoped. But there was a disconcerting moment. One of the stars, Ronald Frankau, was a comedian well known for his 'fruity' humour, as it used to be called, and his educated tones. (He had the additional interest of belonging to a long-established literary family, of Anglo-Jewish origin: it appealed to my taste for improbable connections that his sister, Joan Bennett, should have

---

* There is a brief tribute to him in James Agate's *Ego*, written on the day after he died: 'Tilley's buffoonery sprang from his naive and fumbling mind. It was that timidity, of which every man in his heart knows something, making itself vocal, and we all knew kinship with it.'

been a Cambridge don, and the author of books on George Eliot
and the Metaphysical Poets.) From such a man, I might reasonably
have hoped for something sophisticated. But then he began to
recite a verse monologue, which was supposed to be spoken by an
ear of wheat, and I began to wonder whether he was really all that
funny; and then he came to the punchline – 'My God, I've been
reaped!' – and it was borne in upon me that Sophistication might
not always be all it was cracked up to be.

Still, I wasn't discouraged. The next revue I saw, with Binnie
Hale and Bobby Howes, gave me unqualified pleasure. (What
could have been more Sophisticated than Binnie Hale imitating
Hermione Gingold?) And after that I tried to see all the revues I
could, until my taste for them faded – round about the same time
that they did. (A few years ago, incidentally, I picked up a
programme for *Sauce Tartare* in a junkshop. Studying it, I
discovered that the cast had included, in a series of what must
have been very minor roles, Audrey Hepburn.)

My parents were fond of the West End, too, and our excursions
there for tea, when opportunity allowed, were a high point of the
family weekend. Our most regular ports of call were the old Lyons
Corner Houses – palaces for the middle classes, built on a scale
and with a sumptuousness which I think would be impressive even
now, and which seemed positively Babylonian in comparison with
the drabness of most popular eating establishments at the time. I
revelled in the coloured marble and the chrome, in the mosaics, the
concealed lighting and the art deco motifs. (The black marble of
the men's rooms seemed particularly lordly.) If the other custom-
ers looked even faintly exotic, I fantasised that they led more
interesting lives than they – probably – did. For the price of a mere
afternoon tea, we certainly got our money's worth. But the French
patisserie in Greek Street where we often went instead was even
better. Partly because the place itself had charm – the tiny tearoom
was reached by a rickety staircase from the pastry shop below; still
more because going there involved a foray into Soho.

I caught other glimpses of Soho as well, on expeditions to the
National Gallery, say, or to Foyle's. I knew that, like the West End
itself, it meant many different things: musicians in Archer Street,
cinema offices in Wardour Street, Italian Soho, Jewish Soho (there

were still one or two shop signs in Yiddish), street markets, bohemian pubs, gambling Soho, eccentric Soho. (I more than once caught sight of the notorious Ironfoot Jack, with his cape and with the strange metal frame making up for the missing inches on his right leg. I can well believe Dan Farson when he says, in *Soho in the Fifties*, that he was a dreadful old bore; but at the time – once again, in my early teens – he struck me as mysterious and rather macabre.)

Most of all, to the outside world, Soho meant sex. In an unpermissive age, newspaper stories about 'the square mile of vice' resonated far more than they do today. The whole area, if you were to believe them, was bathed in a lurid glow.

I took no more than a sidelong glance at what was on offer – usually, that is; but I found I couldn't help gazing, every time I passed by, at the window of a bookshop which used to stand in Charing Cross Road, not far from Cambridge Circus. It contained three attractions, which never seemed to change: a large, dusty-looking pink truss, an advertisement for 'Damaroids, The Great British Rejuvenator', and a copy of *Sexual Anomalies and Perversions* by walrus-moustached Magnus Hirschfeld (founder of the Institut für Sexualwissenschaft and, though I naturally didn't know it then, the 'Tante Magnesia' of the homosexual world of pre-Hitler Berlin which Christopher Isherwood wrote about in his memoirs). All in all, it was an uninviting display. Even more than before, I was left feeling that sex was liable to prove problematic in ways I didn't quite understand.

In the summer months we headed for the big parks rather than tearooms. My favourite among them, our collective favourite, was Regent's Park. There was unrivalled satisfaction in the terraces and colonnades, the lake and the rose garden, in its balance between art and nature. But it was especially dear to me on account of a memorable experience – my first visit, at the age of twelve, to the Open Air Theatre. This was also, effectively, my first experience of Shakespeare on the stage, since a previous visit, to an amateur production of *A Midsummer Night's Dream*, had passed me by completely. The play at Regent's Park was *Twelfth Night*; it worked its spell from the opening scene, and carried me along right through. I suppose it was the comedy which got to me first –

and I laughed at least as much at the rougher humours of Sir Toby Belch ('A plague o' these pickle herrings!') as I did at Malvolio. But the poetry reached out to me too, Feste's songs in particular. When I heard 'O mistress mine', I realised that the feeling it inspired welled up from somewhere deep. As we left, with 'When that I was and a little tiny boy' still ringing in my ears, I knew – even though I couldn't have expressed what I felt – that I had been put in possession of something precious, which wasn't going to diminish or go away.

Only one other theatrical occasion during my schooldays left me with quite the same sense of a landmark, or a new beginning. That was three or four years later, when I saw John Gielgud and Diana Wynyard in *Much Ado about Nothing* at the Phoenix Theatre – the first time I had seen Shakespeare in the West End. My memories of the evening are visual rather than verbal. It was a radiant production: I suspect that if I saw it today, I might find it somewhat too smooth. But in what I recall as its high comedy (until the play turns potentially tragic) and its poise, it remains the benchmark to which I can't help reverting when I am disappointed by 'innovative' modern productions – as I frequently am. In the 1990s I saw a production of *Much Ado*, also in the West End, in which one of our best younger actresses made her first entrance as Beatrice stuffing her mouth with a banana, so that you could scarcely hear her words. This is not the way.

The Gielgud *Much Ado* was also notable for another, non-Shakespearean, reason. Bertrand Russell was in the audience that night, sitting two or three rows in front of me. I was impressed by the unostentatious manner in which people stood back to let him pass down the aisle at the interval. And during the last act, when Leonato says

> there was never yet philosopher
> That could endure the toothache patiently,

I saw him turn to his companion and laugh. I thought I *heard* him laugh, too – a dry characteristic chuckle; but he was almost out of earshot, and I may have imagined it.

12

The CLS

I have said almost nothing so far about the City. For anyone with a feeling for London, and 'old London' especially, it had to be the heart of the story, and it impressed itself upon me in many different ways. But during my schooldays it was above all, overwhelmingly, associated with school.

The City of London was a City school in far more than name. It was governed by the City corporation. The Lord Mayor came to present the prizes on speech day, complete with mace-bearer, fur-hatted sword-bearer and the rest of his pantomime retinue. Its badge and motto (*Domine Dirige Nos*) were the City badge and motto, though for good measure it had a second motto as well, *Faber Fabrum Adjuvet* – 'Let craftsman help craftsman', or 'Let carpenter help carpenter': a waggish schoolmasterly reference to John Carpenter, the Town Clerk of London who counted as founder of the school by virtue of provisions he had made in his will in 1442.

This last association was something of a con. The money which Carpenter had left was deflected to other uses, and the school wasn't properly set up until 1837. It was very much a Victorian institution, as its buildings and traditions made plain; and its Victorian flavour (or what survived of it) rather appealed to me. So did the nineteenth-century flavour of the City as a whole, which at the time was was still very marked. I was delighted when I discovered that the main entrance of the great, famous, infamous Stock Exchange was tucked away (in those days) down an alleyway off Bartholomew Lane. And one of the first City landmarks which caught my fancy was Leadenhall Market, with its ornate arcades and fluted pillars, its fancy lettering and City insignia, with office workers stopping off to buy kippers or sausages on the way home and swags of poultry and game hanging up at Christmas time. It is still there, altogether more human and more attractive than the towering new Lloyd's building by which it is now overshadowed.

The school had originally been situated in a turning off Cheapside. In 1880 it moved to an imposing new building with an elaborate Italianate façade ('amazingly unscholastic', according to Pevsner) at the Blackfriars end of the Victoria Embankment. Until you were in the sixth form, you went into it through a side entrance in John Carpenter Street; after that you had the privilege of going up the front steps and through an entrance hall containing busts of Victorian worthies and the marble statue of a youth entitled 'Waiting for His Innings'. Beyond, inside the school, there was a lofty main hall, with stained-glass windows which I used to study during morning assembly – Shakespeare, Spenser and Milton on one side, with Newton, Bacon and Chaucer above them; Homer, Aeschylus and Sophocles on the other side, surmounted by Plato, Thucydides and Herodotus. (The school moved to new premises in the 1980s, and the building was taken over by J.P. Morgan, but the windows and other features have been preserved.)

My father knew something of the City of London before there was any question of my going there. In particular, he had heard of the most distinguished of its former headmasters, Edwin Abbott Abbott. (Abbott was a prodigy, who had become headmaster of the school in 1865, when he was only twenty-six. He was one of the foremost biblical scholars of his time and the author, among much else, of a pioneering Shakespearean grammar, although the one book of his which is still current is the mathematical fantasy *Flatland*.)

Where my father had picked up Abbott's name I'm not sure, but I suspect it was from George Washington Kilner. At all events, when it was decided that I should leave the Perse, the City of London was the first school he thought of, and he managed to arrange an appointment with the headmaster, F.R. Dale. He had been warned that there were no more places available that year, and in principle his mission was hopeless, but when it came to it Dale none the less agreed to accept me – without asking to see me, too, so I can only conclude that my father made out an unusually good case.

I flourished at the City of London, and if Francis Richard Dale had done nothing more than give me a place, I would have reason to remember him with gratitude. But he was a remarkable man on many counts. At the time I arrived at the school he was already sixty-five, and he stayed on for another two years. I don't know whether such an extension, beyond the normal retirement age, was intended as a tribute, but certainly he gave no signs of diminished vigour. He was tall, lean and erect, with white hair, a dark moustache and a yellowish complexion, and he looked as hard as a walnut. He had had an outstanding record in the First World War, serving with the Royal Welch Fusiliers (the regiment Robert Graves writes about in *Goodbye to All That*) and winning both the DSO and the MC. He had also been president of the Classical Association. Kingsley Amis, who was at the CLS, wrote of him in his memoirs that 'to hear him read Greek verse, observing tonic accent, metrical ictus and the run of the meaning all at once, was to be given a distant view of some ideal beauty as well as to marvel at a virtuoso.'

At the same time his scholarship was not so rarefied that he wasn't prepared, year after year, to take junior forms through the rudiments of Latin, using his own textbook, *Paginae Primae*. He had a rich repertory of insults and exhortations to jolly us along ('Village idiot! Doesn't know the way to the Spotted Cow'), and he gave us all Latin names or nicknames. Mine was 'Josephus', and I got a Brownie point for being able to identify the original Josephus, the historian. Only a very discreet Brownie point: he would never have subjected a boy to anything which smacked of flattery.

His immediate predecessor at the City of London had been a clergyman. So had all his other predecessors bar one. But if he had represented something of a break with tradition when he had taken up his post, twenty years on he seemed the very model of a traditionalist. And so he was – if tradition is allowed to include tolerance, good sense and a considerable capacity for innovation.

Dale apart, the teacher who made the most lasting impression was the Reverend C.J. Ellingham (a younger man, though he too had served in the First World War, in the Navy). Ellingham could be formidable – a disapproving look from beneath his dark brows was enough to quell a class – but he also had an easy manner and a charming boyish smile. As a clergyman, he naturally, in those days, wore a dog collar. His main subject was Greek, but he also taught English, with a vigour which didn't preclude attention to detail. When he took us through the Prologue to *The Canterbury Tales*, he was admirable at bringing the pilgrims to life. When he couldn't quite resist scoffing at the five guildsmen in the Prologue, with their prosperous City careers and their ambitious wives ('It is full fair to be yclept "Madame"'), you wondered whether he might not be working off a few subversive feelings about the school's Mansion House and Guildhall connections.

Some of the other members of the staff had almost equally strong personalities – Joe Hunt, for example, an outstanding history teacher, and dandified Dr Law-Robertson, who was a brilliant linguist. Other masters were solid, yet others were eccentric; a few were colourless, but offhand I can't think of one who was an out-and-out dud. And while you could no doubt have found their equivalents at other schools, taken together they formed a distinctive and well-established community. Most of them seemed to have settled into the CLS for life.

The masters' idiosyncrasies were of course ruthlessly and gleefully observed by the boys. It only occurred to me later that most of them were well aware of this, and in general much better at devising counter-insurgency measures than we gave them credit for. For example, Mr Irwin Carruthers – 'Carrots' – was famously incapable of keeping order. I don't suppose, looking back, that the air of polite resignation with which he usually greeted the latest outrage can have been his natural reaction; in reality he must have felt a good deal of anger. But it was a well-judged technique for limiting the damage. After a while it seemed pointless and even rather indecent (boys aren't *that* bad) to provoke him further.

One or two of the teachers seemed to live in their own worlds, and simply went their own sweet way. An extreme case was that of Mr Le Mansois-Field – 'Mickey' Field – who taught French. Much of his energy went into elaborating a fantastic scheme for helping us memorise French irregular verbs. Its fruits could be seen on the blackboard which ran round his classroom, and which was covered with writing, arrows and symbols in a variety of coloured chalks. To help us find our way through this labyrinth, he had also coined a series of shorthand terms, such as 'orange pips', 'naval stripes', 'Follow the Yellow Brick Road'. Perhaps not suprisingly, we tended to emerge from his classes having learned rather more about orange pips and naval stripes than about irregular verbs. But some of his mnemonic devices worked. It was hard to forget the two characters he invented to demonstrate the difference between duty and compulsion, Winston Devoir and Adolf Falloir.

On arriving at the school I had been assigned to the classical side. That meant, among other things, that I spent two or three terms being taught by Percy Copping, who was one of the school's recognised 'characters' – a shrewd man, when he let it show, but often facetious or fatuous in manner. I had a feeling that *he* had a feeling that he was still really a schoolboy, who had been mysteriously transformed into a teacher; I could visualise him being suddenly turned back into a boy, like Mr Bultitude in *Vice Versa*.

Facetiousness can be catching, and he brought out an uncharacteristically frisky vein in the Revd Ellingham. I once saw Ellingham pick up a paper bag which happened to be lying on his desk and put it on Copping's head, saying 'Now you're the king of the castle'. On another occasion he set us a Greek prose about the comic misadventures of a character called Lambanon. *Lambano*, in Greek, means 'I take', or indeed 'I cop'; *lambanon*, the present participle, means 'taking', or indeed 'copping'. Ellingham left us to work that one out for ourselves.

As for what we actually learned, I have forgotten almost all the Greek and the greater part of the Latin. But I subscribe to the consoling belief that Something Rubs Off, and I don't think the time was wasted if I was put in touch, however inadequately, with one of the central traditions of Western culture. There were the living links between Latin and English literature, too. One of our

Virgil textbooks printed Tennyson's poem to 'Roman Virgil' as an appendix, and, though it was hard to reconcile Tennyson's lines with the drudgery aspect of Latin, they did instil a sense of what a proper response to Virgil ought to be. Their impact even survived a piece of schoolboy defacement. Tennyson ends with an allusion to the fact that he had been invited to write the poem by the Vergilian Academy of Mantua – 'I salute thee, Mantovano'. On roughly the same principle which meant that Kennedy's *Shorter Latin Primer* always became a Shortbread Eating Primer, this got changed by some of us into 'I salute thee, Mantovani' (Mantovani the popular musician, famous for the 'cascading effect' of his orchestra's strings). But the joke, such as it was, long ago faded, and I still think that 'To Virgil' is a singularly beautiful poem.

The school had a strong tradition in the teaching of English, going back to the nineteenth century. But I didn't get that much out of my own English lessons (Ellingham aside). When it came to reading, I preferred to follow my fancy; I disliked the whole business of set books and gobbets; I didn't especially respond to the teaching techniques of the senior English master, Geoffrey Clark. In other respects, however, I was fond of Clark (always Geoffrey; he resolutely refused to be Nobbied). There was an aroma of Chelsea and modified bohemianism about him; he would sometimes break off, when he was obviously getting as fed up with the set book as we were, to chat in a brisk non-pedagogic way about (as it might be) the short stories of Angus Wilson, which were then the latest thing. He was no stranger to pubs, as his complexion testified. Once a week he would trot off to give a talk for the BBC World Service at Bush House. Once a year he would produce the school play (*Richard II* one year, *The Apple Cart* the next), which is where he came into his own.

Education is what the other boys teach you as well as what your teachers teach you, and although I still wasn't one for 'best friends', I didn't have much trouble finding sympathetic companions. On the whole I was drawn to boys who seemed sure of themselves, who didn't feel impelled to run with the pack. One such was J.R.H. de S. Honey, a fastidious youth who was famous for using his full set of initials, and for his encyclopaedic knowledge of where eminent people had been to school. Today (we are still friends) he is plain John Honey: Professor Honey, a trenchant writer on linguistics and the scourge of his trendier colleagues. Another friend was a very different proposition. He was what we hadn't yet learned to call laid back, with an impressive drawl and the general air of a nightclub proprietor who had seen it all. One of his great interests was jazz: it was from his lips that I first heard the names of George Melly and Mick Mulligan and his Magnolias. He was also, I imagine, one of the group of boys who achieved a cultural breakthrough by persuading the school librarian to acquire the library's first book on jazz, *Shining Trumpets* by Rudi Blesh.

He made no secret of the fact that he was gay (another as yet unknown term, of course). He told me about some of the gay novelists of the period – Fritz Peters, Rodney Garland – and took me to a dinner party in south London given by the owner of a bookshop with undoubted gay connections. I found this last episode even more interesting than I let on, since at the time I had a crush on another boy, an athlete, which I couldn't bring myself to talk about, but which naturally preyed on my thoughts. What did it mean for the future? I was going through an Aldous Huxley phase, and I was struck by a passage in *Antic Hay* about the hero having fallen in love when he was sixteen with a boy of his own age – 'far more passionately than he had ever done since'. I wondered whether the same couldn't be said of lots of people.

Large tracts of adolescence are best left unrevisited. I still have a lively memory of callow things I did and bumptious things I said, but I don't propose to inflict them on the reader. What made it all worse was that one was so often aware of where one had gone wrong. I remember giving a little grimace when I came across a witticism attributed to a Victorian statesman: 'I like a manly man and a womanly woman, and I'm fond of a girlish girl; what I can't abide is a boily boy.' Not that I had boils – but who can get through adolescence without sometimes suffering their social or psychological equivalent?

One aspect of immaturity, I must admit, was enjoyable, and that was the funny stuff, funny as in 'funny ha-ha': half the time we seemed to be floating on a sea of jokes. Some of our efforts were mad but respectable. For example, there was a boy whose first name was Eliot. One day – this was in the sixth form – several of us were seized by a sudden urge and started bombarding him with terrible half-puns: 'Look out, Eliot, you almost burnt my norton.' 'I must sit down, Eliot, I'm feeling a little gidding.' Most of our humour, however, struck a lower note. I draw a veil over the lewd spoonerisms, the scabrous limericks, the tormented ingenuity devoted to extracting double entendres from the most unpromising material. And then there were the unprintable songs, and the improbable creatures who stalked through them: the captain of the good ship Venus, the four and twenty virgins from Inverness, the monk of great renown, the exceedingly gay caballero.

Some of these last – the songs – were learned at sporting occasions, but rather more were first encountered on field days and other excursions with the cadet force. Sport didn't loom large at the CLS, unless you were keen on it (and my own non-prowess was widely recognised). This was partly because the school sports ground was down in south London, in Grove Park, which involved a fair amount of travel, often coming on top of substantial journeys to school for boys who lived all over London. Under the circumstances, games, beyond a decent minimum, were more a question of *devoir* than *falloir*. But to make up for this, membership of the cadet corps was compulsory. Once or sometimes twice a week the playground became a parade ground.

V.S. Pritchett says in the first volume of his autobiography, *A Cab at the Door*, that he hated the cadets. (He, too, went to a school where they were compulsory.) I can't go quite as far as that, but I certainly found them very tedious. I particularly resented the way in which they blighted Sunday evenings, which had to be partly given over to blancoing and polishing: we wore cadet uniform to school on Mondays. There was one compensation, however. Once I had graduated to the air force section, there were brief opportunities for flying, which was still a novelty in civilian life – ten-minute spins at Heston or Tangmere. And the cadet corps also taught me a useful lesson in the Diversity of Human Nature, and in Not Necesssarily Judging by Appearances.

The school employed a couple of old sweats, Sergeant Cox and Sergeant Stokes, to instruct us in weapon training (why did my rifle always wobble when I presented arms?) and in the schoolboy equivalent of square-bashing. They were men of much the same age, and their names seemed to confirm the superficial impression that they were two of a kind – Box and Cox, peas in a pod. In fact they were very different. Stokes was thoroughly mean. One of his favourite ways of greeting a boy who came under his command was, 'Right, I'm going to maim you' (and he sounded as though he meant it). Cox, on the other hand, though he looked as tough as old boots, was unusually good-natured. I was lucky enough to be assigned to his squad, and he gave proof of his kindness in an incident which still makes me marvel.

We were due to have a big inspection, at which the salute was going to be taken by a very important military personage, General (not yet Field-Marshal) Sir Gerald Templer.* During rehearsals my marching was more than usually uncoordinated, until Cox finally bawled: 'See me afterwards.' When I did go to see him, feeling understandably anxious, he at once said, in an almost apologetic tone, 'I think you'd better not take part in the march past.' I was of course hugely relieved, but I tried not to show it; and I must have succeeded, because he immediately added, in a fatherly manner, 'I know you're disappointed, lad, but you're not up to it. Try not to take it to heart.' A dear man.

It would be wrong to conclude, from the emphasis on the cadet force, that the general atmosphere of the school was regimented or severe. Its traditions were liberal (and indeed Liberal – Asquith was an Old Boy). The fact that it was a day school meant that it had only limited control over pupils' lives, but in addition its ethos, its social mix and even its location all encouraged a certain openness of outlook.

Nowhere was its liberalism more apparent than in its attitude to Jews. It may well have been the only school of its standing in London at that time which didn't maintain, at least unofficially, a Jewish quota or *numerus clausus*. This enlightened attitude went back to the beginning. One of the busts which greeted you in the entrance hall was that of Sir David Salomons, the first Jew to become Lord Mayor of London, and an early benefactor. There

* 'A martinet in appearance and manner, his displeasure – even his presence – was intimidating.' *Dictionary of National Biography.*

had been some outstanding Jewish pupils in the school under Abbott: two of the best known, both of whom went on to become stalwarts of Eng Lit (and to earn knighthoods in the process), were Israel Gollancz and Sidney Lee, the biographer of Shakespeare. And in more recent times the intake of Jewish boys had grown steadily, until they – we – constituted a very substantial minority. As my brother, who also went to the school, once remarked, there was a *minyan* in every classroom (a *minyan* being the quorum of ten worshippers who must be present before Jews can hold full communal prayers).

One consequence was a striking absence of anti-Semitism. For it to have been *completely* absent would have required a miracle. One or two of the masters were rumoured to have a 'thing' about Jews, though if they did they were careful to keep it in check. Some of the boys must have done (but then possibly a few of the Jewish boys had a 'thing' about Gentiles). These are elusive matters, and not, in my view, very important. What *is* important is that of real active threatening prejudice, there was no sign.

A cynic might argue that it was all a question of strength in numbers, and certainly the Jewish boys – most readily identified as we filed out of assembly for Jewish prayers – were a presence to be reckoned with. But the absence of prejudice was only half the story. Relations were also positive. Friendships between Jewish and non-Jewish boys were commonplace.

That having been said, none of us, Jewish or Gentile, were mere neutral depersonalised blanks. We had our own beliefs and affiliations. We had been shaped by our various histories; and it was inevitable that on the whole Jewish boys spent more time with other Jewish boys. In my own case, there was a tilt towards closer Jewish contacts after I had reached my mid-teens, and it became easier for me to visit Jewish friends in the suburbs (which is where almost all of them lived). And then, in my last year at the school, I acquired an especially close friend, a boy called Michael Fox. He subsequently became a leading lawyer in Israel, and circumstances have done a good deal to keep us apart. But our friendship remains firm. So does my respect for him: he is a man of exemplary decency, and a walking refutation of all the hostile jokes about lawyers you ever heard.

13

Joe's Boys

There was a wall in Mile End which I often passed, with three names painted on it in large white letters: 'Bramley, Gaster, Shapiro'. They were the three Communist candidates for a local election. The election had been and gone, the names were still there.

My parents voted Labour, though they had a twinge of regret in 1945, on account of their admiration for Churchill, and I don't think they can ever have been especially ardent Labour supporters. If they had thought it made electoral sense, they would probably have voted Liberal; we were a *News Chronicle* family. But given the practical possibilities, Labour it was.

In the East End of my father's time it would have been hard for anyone with a social conscience not to have had at least some inclination towards the left. Poverty lay all around, memories of worse poverty were still fresh. (The Bryant and May match factory was nearby: a few older people could even recall the epoch-making matchgirls' strike of the 1880s, and the appalling conditions which had given rise to it.)

Not that my father was opposed to capitalism per se. On the contrary, he thought that it was the system best suited to the facts of human nature. And if that implied an unflattering view of human nature, so be it; it was still the only system (to use a slogan of which he had almost certainly never heard) which delivered the goods. That being so, he reserved his condemnation for individual excesses or abuses. He had a particular dislike for East End landlords – for the rent collectors with their leather bags, or rather for the men who employed them. And he certainly didn't see why, within limits, social machinery couldn't be devised to improve existing arrangements. The Health Service was an obvious case in point.

These were matters for discussion, however, for negotiation, persuasion and peaceful adjustment: the politics of give and take. But there were also the politics of life and death, meaning primarily Nazism and Communism. And once Nazism had been defeated, Communism became the central issue.

By 1946 or 1947, as the Cold War deepened, most people would have agreed. But in Mile End the question had moved to the top of the agenda almost as soon as the Second World War ended. In the 1945 General Election, the Mile End division returned the Communist candidate, Phil Piratin. The following year, as though to show this wasn't a flash in the pan, the Communists won the two Mile End seats on the LCC.

My father's antipathy to Communism went back a long way: it must, I think, have had its origins in his recoil from the ferocity of the Communists' attack on religion. But that was only his starting point. It gave him the key which enabled him to take a critical attitude to Communism in general, and common sense and an ability to see things as they were did the rest. He wasn't deceived by Stalinist propaganda in the thirties, still less by the black farce of the Moscow Trials. He recognised the purges as the monstrous product of a monstrous regime.

At the same time, Jewish issues remained an especially sore point, all the more so because so many Jews were members of the party or fellow-travellers. (It was no secret that it was Jewish voters in Mile End who had put Piratin in.) Disputes over Communism often had the added edge of a family quarrel – a complicated quarrel, since Communists claimed to be the most reliable and effective anti-fascists, and hence the most reliable and effective defenders of Jewish interests. My father wasn't convinced (he thought that they were Communists first and last, that the anti-fascism was incidental), and events, as far as he was concerned, had borne him out. He once told me that shortly after the outbreak of war he had given a lift to a pair of young Jewish Communists, friends of a relative, but that he had asked them to get out of the car when they started defending the Molotov–Ribbentrop pact. From what I know of him, he probably set them down at a convenient point: he wouldn't have wanted to leave them stranded. But I was impressed by the depth of anger he must have felt, given how mild and non-confrontational he usually was.

Once Russia was in the war, public criticisms were shelved. Enthusiasm for things Soviet became the order of the day, and the Soviet authorities were especially adept at playing on it among Jews. The most notable event in this respect was the official visit paid to London in 1943 by Solomon Mikhoels, director of the Moscow Yiddish State Theatre, and the Yiddish poet Itzik Feffer. Their presence elicited an enormous response from British Jews, including many who could by no stretch be called pro-Communist. So, naturally enough, did the achievements of the Red Army. I was related by marriage to a Yiddish poet called Joseph Hillel Lowy, who came to England with his family just before the war. He was a quiet, dignified man; his longest poem was an account of his father, who had been a *sofer* (a scribe expert at writing out Scrolls of the Law), and as far as I know he didn't normally concern himself with politics. A few years ago, however, I learned by chance that early in 1945 he had published a poem to mark the liberation of Warsaw and Cracow (his home town), entitled '*Zay Gebentsht Du Marshal Stalin*' – 'Blessings on you, Marshal Stalin'. It is a sad thought, though his sentiments have to be set in context: he was writing in the era of the Big Three, when 'Uncle Joe' was being extolled on every side.

I don't know exactly what my father felt about the avuncular marshal and his regime during the war years. I am sure that he was overwhelmingly preoccupied with the war itself, and its dreadful consequences; beyond that, my guess is that he put his reservations about Communism on hold, but retained an inner scepticism.

When I first became interested in such matters, in the early post-war period, I can hardly have failed to absorb some of his attitudes. Even so, I remember being shocked by an article about Russia in *Newsweek* which I read during my first year at the Perse, in 1946 or 1947. It wasn't the criticisms themselves which surprised me – I knew enough to know that Russia wasn't sacrosanct – but the hard, unyielding tone in which they were delivered. Could it really be that we were no longer allies?

Before long, like everyone else, I had adjusted to the idea. By the time of the Berlin Airlift, in 1948, it was a clear case of Us against Them. Yet as my political awareness grew, there was a corner of my mind in which I remained undecided about Communism, or at any rate intrigued by it.

This was partly for what might be called family reasons. I had a number of relatives, on my mother's side, who were Communist sympathisers. None of them were people we saw very often; when we did, relations were perfectly cordial, which probably means that there was a tacit understanding that political disagreements should not be pushed too far. But I heard something of their views, even so, and saw something of what they were reading. They were my introduction, not perhaps to the doctrines of Communism, but to its culture and mindset.

I had an aunt who had gone through a Communist phase, which she may have left behind: she never spoke about it. But she had a small shelf of 'serious' books, which I sometimes sneaked a look at. Apart from *The Physiology of Sex*, by Kenneth Walker, which she had put in brown paper wrappers, they were all political. The ones I dipped into were *The Socialist Sixth of the World*, by the notorious 'Red Dean' of Canterbury, Hewlett Johnson, and *Serving My Time*, a memoir by Harry Pollitt. In another relative's flat there were copies of *Germany Puts the Clock Back*, by Edgar Ansell Mowrer, and *Red Star over China*, by Edgar Snow. I got the two Edgars mixed up, or ran them together: Communism and anti-fascism still seemed cut out of the same cloth.

My idea of Communism was derived less from books, however, than from the *Daily Worker*. I read it whenever I came across a copy. I got to know some of its regular features: two which I always seized on were the pocket cartoons by Gabriel and, rather oddly, the latest reports of the Fighting Fund (cash contributions from readers) organised by a woman called Barbara Niven. I became familiar with the names of its correspondents: Sam Russell, who reported from Moscow; Derek Kartun, who wrote strident attacks on America; Alan Winnington, who was to cover the Korean War from the North Korean side. And beyond them there were the great men: Bill Rust, the editor; Haldane the scientist; Harry Pollitt; and, greatest of all, R. Palme Dutt, *éminence rouge* and supposedly austere razor-sharp theoretician. (A few years later, when I met Dutt in the late Raphael Samuel's rooms in Balliol, he didn't seem razor-sharp at all, just immensely pleased with himself. I recently learned from Alison Macleod's excellent book *The Death of Uncle Joe* that 'in the *Daily Worker* office, where he seldom set foot, he was regarded with derision'.)

Much of the fascination which the *Worker* held for me was that of a looking-glass world in which customary values were reversed – something which could be diverting as long as one didn't consider the consequences too closely. But I also had an occasional suspicion that ultimately the Communists might turn out to be right. There were people with money, and there were people without money. It seemed wrong. Not a very profound thought, nor one that would necessarily lead one into the arms of the CP. But I wasn't being consistent, or trying to think things through: I am talking about scattered adolescent impulses.

These impulses were reinforced by much of my reading, especially fiction. I had reached the age at which one hopes that novels are going to teach one what life is all about, and without having any particular plan I found myself drawn to a number of books with a strong left-wing slant. They were mostly American, and mostly rather old-fashioned (the other side of my taste for reading about J.P. Morgan or the Duponts). I must have read half a dozen novels by Upton Sinclair, for instance: I was shocked – a fair measure of my innocence – by a scene in one of them in which a wealthy Bostonian is stopped for speeding but waved on as soon as the cop has recognised who he is and accepted a small gift. Another enthusiasm (I didn't recognise its obvious Communist provenance) was Cedric Belfrage's novel *Promised Land*, the first unvarnished account of Hollywood I had encountered. And I was prompted, perhaps by memories of Edward G. Robinson in *The Sea Wolf*, to get Jack London's *The Iron Heel* out of the library. It made a strong impression – although incongruously, I didn't blench at its vision of a bloodstained quasi-Marxist apocalypse, but I was shaken (another measure of innocence) by its dismissal of charity, under capitalism, as 'a mere bandaging of the wound'.

I don't believe I was ever in real danger of succumbing to the totalitarian temptation. As my ideas became more focused, and as the novelty of Communism wore off, I began to find the whole far Left mentality chilling. It didn't need any great wit to see that Communists and fellow-travellers were wrong about Russia, and much else, and that they were ready to swallow the most blatant lies. What took longer to grasp was that they were driven, above all, by the love of power. There were countless apologists ready to argue that, on the contrary, they were men of good will: they might be overzealous, but that only made them 'liberals in a hurry'. And no doubt many of them had embraced Communism in the first instance through honourable motives; through compassion, or a sense of justice. But once they had been sucked into the system, power was what it was about.

What did this power mean in practice, in Britain – not for party officials, who were already exercising some, but for the rank and file, for fellow-travellers, for people like my relatives? A few, at least, must have had dreams of one day being members of a new ruling class – of throwing their weight about. Why not, with History, and the Soviet Union, on their side? But mostly, I think, it was a question of feeling intellectually superior (not to say smug). They had *seen through* conventional appearances, to the realities and secret structures underneath. And that meant that they had seen through everyone who disagreed with them, or who hadn't caught up with them – which, as other movements besides Marxism have shown, is something that can confer a sense of power on the most unremarkable people.

Once this negative view had begun to evolve, there were books to speed it on its way. I didn't read *Animal Farm* or *Nineteen Eighty-Four* or *Darkness at Noon* until well into the 1950s. I almost felt by then (wrongly, of course) that I didn't need to, since Orwell's essays had already made a lasting impression; so, to a lesser degree, had Koestler's contribution to the symposium *The God that Failed*; so had a number of other books. One whose impact I especially recall was Margarete Buber's memoir *Under Two Dictators*. (The English translation was published – to his credit, by Victor Gollancz – in 1949.) The author was the wife of a leading German Communist who had accompanied her husband to Russia in the 1930s. In 1937 he had been arrested, and disappeared. She had been arrested the following year, sent to a slave camp in Siberia, and then handed over to the Gestapo in 1940 and sent to Ravensbrueck: this was during the period of the Nazi–Soviet friendship pact. Of the two hells she describes, the Nazi was undoubtedly the worse. But the Soviet hell was no less a hell for that; and who had been responsible for her ending up in Ravensbrueck, anyway?

Not that you needed books to get a general picture of what was happening. It was enough to read the papers, or listen to the radio; and once or twice I heard something like first-hand testimony. One of my father's patients was a Jew who had been born in Romania, and who had gone back there for a visit after the war, to see whether he could find out what had happened to his relatives. They had all been murdered; he was not someone likely to underestimate the importance of opposition to fascism, from whatever quarter it came. But he was still horrified by current conditions in Romania, under the new Communist regime. His exact words, as my father reported them, were, 'People ought to thank God they live in this country. When I got back I wanted to kneel down and kiss the pavement.'

The best-known figure in the Romanian government at that time, apart from the prime minister, was the fearsome figure of Anna Pauker. She was the daughter of a rabbi, which somehow (as far as we were concerned) made things worse – all the more so because this was the period during which Stalin's policies towards Jews took an uglier turn. And though the Jewish issue, as my father would have unhesitatingly agreed, was only one item in the catalogue of Stalinist infamy, we could hardly have failed to be exceptionally aware of it. When Soviet spokesmen denounced 'cosmopolitans', for instance, we didn't need to be told whom they had in mind.

One of the many prominent victims of Stalin's anti-Semitism was the theatre director Solomon Mikhoels. In 1948, five years after he had been fêted in London, he was shot down by the secret police on a street in Minsk: they subsequently ran a lorry over his body to make it look like an accident. (As Khrushchev wrote in his memoirs, 'they killed him like beasts'.) And in 1952 Mikhoels' companion on the visit to London, Itzik Feffer, was executed, along with the other leading Yiddish writers in Russia, after having been accused – a bizarre charge even by Stalinist standards – of plotting to set up a secessionist state in the Crimea.

Throughout this period, as far as I know, very few Jewish Communists in Britain defected from the party. What made the situation even more galling was that those who stayed, or who remained fellow-travellers, were often gifted people. (It would have been easy, in fact – though it wouldn't have been true – to create the impression that to be an intellectual or an artist you had to be on the left, and pretty far to the left at that. To take only one instance, most of the Jewish actors from the East End who made a name for themselves after the war began their careers under Communist auspices, at the Unity Theatre (and some of them retained their early political outlook to the last). There was no non-Communist equivalent to the Unity.

In the summer of 1950 we spent a couple of weeks at Clacton – our last bucket-and-spade seaside holiday. A Jewish accountant was staying at the same hotel, a man who could not talk to you for more than a minute or two without letting you know that his sympathies lay on the far left. We chatted to him a few times about this and that; then he and my father fell into conversation about the Korean War, which had broken out a few weeks before. My father supported American-led intervention, he naturally didn't; they grew quite sharp with each other, until he said, 'Well, if you're willing to let your boy die fighting for the Americans, I'm not.' After that, our exchanges with him were limited to a stiff 'Good morning' and 'Good evening'.

Two or three years later I got to know his son at Oxford. He was quiet, studious, a good linguist and a skilled translator. When it came to politics he was very much his father's son, although he fished in deeper waters: his particular hero was the Marxist critic George Lukacs. Eventually, he became associated with the group which launched the *Universities and Left Review*, subsequently the *New Left Review*, in the wake of Khrushchev's denunciation of Stalin – the group whose members transformed themselves from pillars of the Old Left into founders of the New Left, with remarkably little pause for reflection.

There are those who believe that this is all ancient history, that in Britain, at least, the Communists accomplished nothing. I don't agree. Their political legacy may have been zero; their social and cultural legacy, as mediated through their New Left successors, has been immense. Nor can I buy the view that most of them were innocents, who didn't really know what they were doing – that, as somebody once said, they were 'more gauche than sinister'. They may have *chosen* not to know, but that is not the same thing.

A few years ago I saw two of my *communisant* cousins, elderly men by then, greet each other at a family gathering with clenched fist salutes – as a little joke, for old times' sake. I simply smiled – who wants to make a fuss on such occasions? And indeed, in the context of a suburban tea party it all seemed rather foolish and inconsequential. But later, looking back, I gave a slight shudder. Their gesture was trivial; but at the other end of the spectrum, at however far a remove, lay the Great Terror and the Gulag.

14

Choices

In the old days every self-respecting Jewish family had at least one Uncle Morrie. We had three, and between them they covered a nice span of Jewish possibilities.

One – he was actually a great-uncle – was a minor official of the United Synagogue, with a beaming countenance and a set of well-tried jocular catchphrases: at family gatherings, there usually came a point where he would turn to the table where the food was spread out and say, 'Now where are the doings?' Another, also a great-uncle, was the oldest of the family's Communists. As a schoolboy I once tried to get a rise out of him by telling him that I had heard that there was a particularly good book about the French Revolution by Edmund Burke. He immediately shot back, 'Edmund Burke called working people "the swinish multitude", and that's all I need to know about him.' Since my own knowledge of Burke at the time was virtually non-existent, I was completely floored.

The Uncle Morrie who meant the most to me was a real uncle, my father's younger brother. I was partly impressed by him because he had a striking physical presence: he was unusually tall, much taller than anyone else in the family, with a long strong face to match. He also seemed to me to have style. Possibly this didn't mean much more, in my boyish view of things, than the fact that he was rumoured to have always taken taxis (which I had been brought up to consider a luxury), even in the days when he couldn't afford them, and that by the time I knew him he and his family lived in a smart flat near Regent's Park. But he was undoubtedly intelligent and independent-minded as well, and he had been determined from early on to get away from the more constricting aspects of family life.

One route he took was to anglicise himself, more than anyone else in my father's family. He changed the spelling of his name to Grose, because it was more English; he sent his daughter, who was about my age, to Bedales. At the same time he was quite assertive about being Jewish, especially in the face of rising anti-Semitism, and he also responded strongly to the attraction of Zionism. It was his Zionist impulse which eventually won out.

He was an accountant by profession, and not long after he had qualified, around 1930, he went out to Palestine to work for the Palestine Electric Corporation. The founder and manager of the corporation, Pinhas Rutenberg, was one of the most interesting personalities involved in building up the Yishuv, the Jewish community in Palestine. An engineer, he had also been a leading member of the Russian Socialist Revolutionary Party; as a minister in Kerensky's government in 1917, he had consistently advocated taking whatever measures were needed to head off Lenin. In Palestine, his work on hydro-electric power, beginning in the early twenties, had helped to transform the economy. He developed political ambitions there, too, in which he was less successful; but my uncle greatly admired the technocratic, businesslike side of his character.

While in Palestine my uncle got married. His wife came from a well-known family, originally from the Polish town of Bialystok, and considerably higher up the social scale than ours, as we were more than once reminded. She was a trim, petite woman; my uncle towered over her, and I am told that in the early days of their marriage they were known as the *lulav* and the *esrog* (the tall palm branch and the small citron carried by Jews on the festival of Tabernacles).

Towards the end of the thirties he returned to London with his family. I didn't see much of them on account of the war, and after the war they went back to what was soon to be the State of Israel. My uncle didn't have any links with the Labour Party, which was the dominant force in Israeli politics at the time, but he eventually found a niche as secretary of the Chamber of Commerce in Haifa.

When I stayed with him on my first visit to Israel, in 1953, he seemed to be engaged in daily battles with the leader of the local dock-workers' union. He was also ill, and he died a few years later, still in his forties.

My father was fond of him. So was my mother; and they both respected him. We were close, in other words, to someone who had chosen to live his life in Israel. Didn't it follow that we felt close to Israel itself? Wouldn't we have felt close to it, anyway?

These are questions I find it impossible to answer with a straight yes or no. As a Jewish enterprise, the Yishuv was something my family had wished well. As a refuge for Jewish victims of persecution, it was something they had naturally supported. The Jewish resettlement of Palestine had been brought home to them in many different ways, both private and public. But it had never been a central part of their existence: they certainly weren't anti-Zionist, but they weren't Zionists either.

That much is what I was told, or what I deduced. By the time I had a clearer picture of what was happening, from 1946 or so, their attitude had begun to change. The period leading up to the establishment of Israel brought new emotions into play – anxiety, anger, admiration – or at any rate greatly heightened old ones. These feelings were inevitably coloured by the revelations, still very recent, of what had happened during the war; the whole situation was also rendered more painful by what everyone perceived as the clear pro-Arab, anti-Jewish bias of the Attlee government. Ernest Bevin's role was particularly troublesome. Under other circumstances he would have been a hero – for his achievements as Minister of Labour during the war, for his general performance as Foreign Secretary. As it was, nothing did more to produce a closing of the ranks than his notorious remark that 'Jews must not try to get to the head of the queue'. (He was talking about restrictions on Jewish immigration to Palestine.) Not only was the remark made in the context of concentration-camp survivors and Displaced Persons; it was also, so to speak, unnecessary. Realpolitik alone would not have dictated it; indeed, realpolitik left to itself would probably have shed a few crocodile tears. It felt like an emanation of pure prejudice.

When Israel became an independent state in May 1948, we

joined in the general rejoicing. (In a fairly sedate fashion, however. Lou and Harry, the boys next door, stayed up most of the night celebrating with friends; we went round and had a drink with them.) Immediately after that, euphoria gave way to apprehension about the outcome of the Arab–Israeli war; after that there were excitements, good moments, bad moments and readjustments. For a year or two, the sense of sheer novelty was still strong. I can recall the thrill we got from driving over to Manchester Square to see the building, near the Wallace Collection, which housed the first Israeli embassy. Everyone was proud, too, that the first Israeli ambassador, Dr Eliash, was both distinguished and distinguished-looking. And then, Jews being Jews, there were the jokes. (I quote one, purely for its period flavour: 'A miracle! For the first time in two thousand years Jews are driving their own trains!')

Israel was now a fact of life (except for those who wanted to destroy it). For Jews, or most Jews, it was a large fact. Before Israel became a state, my parents hadn't, as far as I know, contributed to the Jewish National Fund. They now made an annual donation to its much more streamlined fund-raising successor. Yet the change was only relative. For all its importance, Israel wasn't at the heart of their concerns, any more than the Yishuv had been. They never saw their future, or that of their children, as lying anywhere but in England.

My own enthusiasm for the new state was stronger than theirs. I was young, I was under the influence of contemporaries, I wanted to see the country for myself. I sometimes wondered, too, about going to live there. But only fitfully; and when I encountered genuine, 100 per cent Zionists – people who had settled in Israel, or were planning to – I often found myself backing away from their rigidity and dogmatism, from the demands which they laid on me as a potential recruit. I was even slightly put out by the fact that the textbook from which I tried, not very successfully, to learn modern Hebrew was called *Hebrew for All* in English, but *Ivri, L'mud Ivrit!* – 'Hebrew, Learn Hebrew!', which sounded so very much more peremptory – in Hebrew itself. (The author of the book, who ran a couple of summer schools which I attended, was anything but peremptory in person. He was an affable Scottish schoolteacher, with a strong Glaswegian accent and a fondness for the essays of Charles Lamb.)

At the same time I recognised that states are only likely to be built by men and women who make hard demands, both on themselves and on others; and I was equally troubled by the apparent iron logic of Arthur Koestler, who began arguing at this period that, now that Jews had their own state, they were faced with a simple choice. If they wanted to remain Jews, they should go to Israel; otherwise they should forget the whole thing. The only reply I could think of was that life wasn't like that, that people are inconsistent. And so it has proved in the case of Israel and the Jews. But I must admit that Koestler's argument can still ruffle me. At the Passover service, which ends with the prayer 'Next year in Jerusalem', I have sometimes imagined his ghost looking down and asking, 'Why pray, when you can buy a ticket from El Al?'

My first visit to Israel, which lies beyond the scope of this memoir, took place when I was eighteen. My parents saw me off at the station (in those days you went by train and boat), and just before we said goodbye I had a distinct impression that my father wanted to say to me, 'Don't stay there. Be sure to come back.' In the event, he needn't have worried. The visit was a success. My commitment to Israel (though not to everything that every Israeli government does, of course) was strengthened. I met some admirable people, and had some stirring experiences. But I came back.

The troubles in Palestine produced smaller troubles in Britain. Much smaller, but disagreeable enough.

I remember all too clearly one summer morning when I was twelve, picking up the morning paper and seeing a picture on the front page – the two British sergeants who had been hanged in an orange grove by the Irgun as a reprisal for the execution of three of its members. That episode provoked several days of anti-Jewish disturbances, in London and the provinces. And there were lesser incidents which still sowed ample ill feeling, such as the notorious statement by the Hollywood writer Ben Hecht that every time a British soldier was killed in Palestine there was a song in his heart.

('What made him say it?' my father wanted to know. 'What good did he think it would do?') Those were difficult times for British Jews. The great majority of them condemned the killing of the sergeants. Most of them, if pressed, would have agreed that an angry public reaction was inevitable, that it would have been inevitable anywhere. But in practice it was often hard to say where outrage ended and anti-Semitism began. Feelings were tense. Hostility came out into the open.

I can only recall witnessing one incident myself. A few of us were fooling around on the edge of a playing field. There had been some talk about Palestine; then a non-Jewish boy suddenly pinned a Jewish boy down and said to him, 'You killed Christ.' It was the first time I had heard those words uttered, and I was not so much afraid – the victim threw his tormentor off, and there was no further rough-housing – as incredulous. (The writer Erich Heller, who was much more genial than you might suppose if you only knew him from such austere books as *The Disinherited Mind*, once told me that when *he* first heard those same words, as a schoolboy in Central Europe, he wanted to reply, 'No, it wasn't me, it was the Cohen boys down the road.')

Anti-Jewish feeling which was specifically associated with the Palestine issue gradually subsided. It didn't entirely disappear, but by the 1950s the climate was very different. Nor, for all its unpleasantness, did it seriously hamper the social and economic advances which were being made by Jews during the same period. And anti-Semitism in general, as a new post-war generation came forward, was in decline.

In my own case, as I have made clear, it wasn't a practical problem. Alongside any direct experience – or non-experience – of anti-Semitism, however, there was also the knowledge that it existed. That knowledge had inevitably taken on a darker aspect since the war, so much so that I felt it important not to go too far, not to equate minor anti-Semitism (the golf club variety) with major anti-Semitism. But the two couldn't be altogether divorced, either.

Meanwhile, pockets of vicious prejudice were still apparent, above all with the post-war Mosleyite revival. One of our routes to north London for weekend family visits took us past Ridley Road

in Dalston – famous for its big street market, which was heavily
Jewish (my boxing-promoter hero Jack Solomons had his fish-
monger's business there), but also a site much favoured by fascists
for their open-air meetings, and the scene of frequent pitched
battles when those meetings were disrupted by the Jewish ex-
servicemen of the 43 Group. We would make a small detour on
our journeys through the area if there was any hint of trouble, or if
we saw police vans waiting in the side streets; but one drizzly
Sunday we found ourselves held up while a fascist parade marched
by with an escort of mounted police. There was that jolt you
always get when you see something nasty for the first time,
however many times you may have heard about it. Perhaps seeing
is the only form of *completely* believing.

Ugly though the post-war Mosleyites were, and frightening
though individual fascists could be face to face, collectively they
represented less a threat than a reminder – of what had happened
in Nazi-occupied Europe; of what could have happened in Britain;
of how things had looked before the war. In retrospect, it can be
seen that the danger posed by Mosley in the 1930s, of which I had
heard a good deal, was exaggerated: his fortunes had been in
decline by 1937 or 1938. But that retrospect is supplied by the
outcome of the war. At the time, his essential menace had been the
reflected menace of Hitler. It was not so much a matter of votes (of
which he never got many), but of the fact that he was part of an
international pattern, and the fear that he might be riding the
wave of history. After 1945, however, he was on his own, and by
the end of the forties, with his revived movement fizzling out, he
was a back number.

Around that time – 1950 is as close a date as I can get – I had a
little reminder that, Mosley or no, pathological anti-Semitism lived
on. We had been spending the afternoon in Kensington Gardens.
My father and I had gone off for a stroll; we had sat down for a
moment on a bench in the Broad Walk when a couple came and
sat beside us. He was a small man with a slightly grubby and
indefinably unwholesome look – the kind of man who even in
those innocent days would probably have been turned down on
sight if he had tried to become a scoutmaster. His wife (as I assume
she was) seemed a mere mouse. Almost at once they started having

a violently anti-Semitic conversation, with the man doing most of the talking and woman egging him on. It went on for about a minute – we were transfixed – until he said, 'I think they should all be towed out to sea in a ship and drowned.' Then we got up and walked away.

I was so naive, or possibly so reluctant to face the truth, that it was a long while before I realised that the couple had obviously spotted that we were Jewish, and that the conversation had been conducted specifically for our benefit. What I did find myself wondering, immediately afterwards, was why we hadn't said anything, and why I hadn't been ready to hit the man if he had replied with fresh abuse. It wouldn't have taken much courage: he was a puny specimen. Had my father and I, for a minute, assumed the role of passive victims? I felt renewed admiration for the tough tactics of the 43 Group.

One could argue, I suppose, that the couple were too feeble to be worth bothering about. But no doubt many Nazis would have looked similarly feeble if Hitler hadn't given them their chance. The old poison was still there. One could only hope that it would never again be put to use.

Jews growing up after the war (not all of them, I need hardly say) felt under a strong obligation to affirm their Jewishness. Attempting to deny it seemed peculiarly base. I recall a friend, who was in most respects highly susceptible to the charms of assimilation, saying to me, 'I don't want to be the one in whom the whole thing ends.' Not that it would have done, whatever he had got up to; putting the matter that way was an oblique statement of solidarity.

In my own case, a sense of solidarity helped to sustain my religious beliefs in the face of adolescent wavering. But my doubts didn't go away, and one incident in particular helped to underline them as nothing quite had before.

Among the family left behind in Poland my father had a cousin, about ten years younger than him, called Moishe Roitenburg. By the time I first heard of him he was Maurice – pronounced in the French fashion (so I can't claim him as another Morrie). Unable to fulfil his ambition of becoming a doctor in Poland, he had studied in France and stayed on there after qualifying. For a time, I believe, he worked for a miners' union, treating industrial diseases. When my parents were in Paris on their honeymoon, he had shown them round, and after the war he had re-established contact. During the occupation he had inevitably been in deadly danger; *juif* was bad enough, *juif polonais* was worse. Initially he had gone into hiding in the woods, but after that he had been protected by French colleagues. He was now married to a non-Jewish girl, and working at a hospital at Evreux, in Normandy.

On our first post-war visit to Paris, in 1949, he came up from Evreux to have lunch with us. To my inexperienced eyes, he looked very French, but that was probably on account of the thick black frames of his glasses and the cut of his suit. Before lunch, my father made it clear that we still observed *kashrut*, the dietary laws; Maurice may have made it clear in turn (I'm not sure) that he didn't. At the restaurant, he took charge of the menu; he first ordered the omelettes or fish that we had dutifully asked for, and then added with a flourish, '*Et pour moi, veau au pot*'.

The moment passed without comment, and I didn't think there was going to be any fallout. But when Maurice had left, and we had got back to our hotel, my father was furious. Not only that: his features assumed a jeering expression I had never seen before, and he repeated two or three times, in an attempt at mimicry, '*Et pour moi, veau au pot; et pour moi, veau au pot.*' I kept quiet, which is just as well, because I found his reaction detestable. To get so worked up over such a small thing! To make no allowance for what Maurice had gone through during the war! And wasn't the whole food taboo childish and primitive anyway?

Today, it seems to me that both men must have been under pressures I can only guess at. Maurice, after all, struck me as amiable and polite, not someone who would normally have been indifferent to causing offence. And even at the time I had to concede, on reflection, that my father, given how angry he was, had actually shown considerable restraint: things would have been much worse if he had said anything while Maurice was still there. I calmed down, and detestation faded. But distaste remained.

My father once said to me that no virtue was more important than tolerance. The remark hadn't impressed me quite as much as it should have done, as a general sentiment, because I couldn't help reflecting that tolerance was something in which Jews had a vested interest. What did impress me, however, living with him and observing him, was the extent to which he lived up to his watchword in practice. He was patient, forbearing and slow to condemn. He got on with people; he took it for granted that we had to live in a world where there were, in the great phrase, 'all sorts and conditions of men'. Even in matters of religion, he was often prepared to relax the rules. But religion was also his sticking point. Every so often he would take a stand which was not only unyielding but, from my point of view, unreasonable as well.

I think there was another, unspoken issue lurking behind the *veau au pot* incident, the question of intermarriage. Part of my own heated reaction may well have been the result of picturing myself in a similar situation. I dreaded the explosion there would be if one day I were to announce that I was marrying someone who wasn't Jewish. And although my guess is that my parents would eventually have come round (my mother much more readily than my father), there would still have been enormous distress – and embarrassments and long boring arguments, too. But I also knew, without quite wanting to spell it out to myself, that if the problem ever arose I would follow my own path.

The meeting with Maurice was an undoubted milestone, but it would be quite misleading to portray my adolescence as one long process of emancipation from religion. My inner feelings fluctuated; my outward commitment became, if anything, more obvious. As my circle of Jewish friends widened, I spent more time with people who simply took the main framework of Jewish communal life for granted. In particular, Michael Fox introduced me to a small youth movement, the Study Groups, which suited my needs very well for a year or two. It was religious, in moderation; it encouraged an interest in Israel without being burdened with an ideology. And it was fun. A good deal of our energy went into writing skits and comic songs. Michael wrote one number which I thought was brilliant of its kind, and still do – a parody of a hit song of the period by Les Compagnons de la Chanson, 'Les trois cloches', recounting the rise of an *alrightnik* who began life as little Moishele, transmuted himself into Maurice Conway and ended up in full splendour as Sir Maurice Conway-Ferguson. We performed it, along with some other songs, at a student concert in Israel in 1953, and we were warmly received with one conspicuous exception – the guest of honour, Golda Meir (then a cabinet minister), sat stony-faced throughout. She was not amused.

Much of my continuing readiness to believe, and to pray, was based on loyalty – loyalty to the 'little platoon' into which I had been born, and to the larger tradition of which it constituted a tiny part. But religion retained my allegiance on broader grounds, too. To put it minimally, I didn't think that terms such as soul, spirit and holiness were meaningless words. It seemed to me that without the realm of religious experience, life would be a thinner and poorer thing, and that it supplied the poetry of collective existence, as rationalism never could. Nobody had yet written an Elegy in a Country Crematorium.

These were arguments, or promptings, in favour of religion in general, rather than of any one religion. But religion in general was nowhere to be found. There were only religions; and although in principle, in an open society, one was free to choose among them, in practice one's choice had been made by history. (I might add that history had also instilled in me a tenderness towards the Church of England – towards its liturgy and literature and traditions, rather than its actual creed. The decline of the Church in recent years has saddened me, although I suppose a believer might say that I am confusing religious judgements with cultural or aesthetic ones.)

Meanwhile, the forces tugging me towards unbelief remained strong. I was never much drawn to philosophy, but when I was, it was the hard reasoners who attracted me, rather than the pseudo-theologians. One of the few philosophers I could read for pleasure was David Hume; and had I known it then, I would have been struck by the truth of Heine's observation that as soon as religion solicits the aid of philosophy, it is doomed. Not that this was the end of the matter. There were more things in heaven and earth, etc.; religion was about faith rather than reason, and there was even a perverse satisfaction in yielding to its unreasonableness. I was thrilled, at the age of fifteen or so, when I first came across Tertullian's *credo quia impossibile*, 'I believe because it is impossible'. But my enthusiasm soon cooled. I didn't have the temperament to subsist on a diet of impossibility for very long.

In the end, here as in other respects, I wanted the best of both worlds. 'Ambiguity' became a blessed word; the fact that so many things contained their opposite was on the whole a comfort. I could have said, with Cyril Connolly, that I believed in 'the Either, the Or and the Holy Both'. In practice, however, choices had to be made, and in practice I edged away from both prayer and observance. (I gave up my final food taboos on that first trip to Israel – in Jerusalem, no less.)

But there were still limits. To have made a clean break with Judaism would have felt like making a clean break with myself. Wavering became a way of life, and by the age of eighteen I had settled, or seemed to have settled, for a world of token observance and demisemi-belief.

My father died when I was twenty-five. He had had a coronary, which was almost an occupational disease of GPs in those days, two years before, and his smoking can't have helped. The second time round, he took to his bed for a week or so. Then, when he felt worse, he went into the London Hospital, where so many of his patients had been sent in their time.

During the last few days at home he managed to read a little. There were two books by his bedside. One was a copy of *The Young Melbourne*, by David Cecil. (What would they have made of that in Gorokhov?) 'He writes beautifully,' he said. The other was Irving Howe's anthology of Yiddish short stories, which I had brought back for him from America. He read a story by the poet Chaim Grade, in which the central character was a follower of the religious movement known as Musar, and it set him reminiscing. Only briefly; he was tired. But he spoke for a moment or two about the founder of the movement, the nineteenth-century rabbi Israel Salanter, and of the emphasis which the Musarists put on morality – on self-examination and good deeds.

In the hospital he was much weaker, and often in pain. The last conversation we had, as opposed to exchanging a few words, was about Khrushchev, Eisenhower and the shooting down of the U-2 spy plane, which had just taken place: he was worried about the consequences. ('They wouldn't be mad enough to start a war?') A day or two later, the young doctor who came out from behind the screen round his bed didn't really have to say anything: we could read the bad news in his face.

Of the funeral which followed, I remember very little: it was simply something to be got through. One incident does stand out, though. On the way back from the cemetery someone introduced me to a small, smiling old woman, and told me that she had been my father's wet nurse. It seemed incredible, a visitation from a world which was impossibly remote. But later I reflected that she need not have been more than eighty, and could even have been a year or two less.

Afterwards we 'sat shivah', observing the traditional seven days of mourning, while relatives and friends visited us at home. In some ways I found this a strain. Reciting Kaddish, the mourner's prayer, seemed profoundly right. So did lighting a candle. But an elderly relative (not even a close one) took charge of the proceedings and insisted we cover the mirrors, which as far I was concerned introduced a note of spooky superstition; and some of the conversations I was obliged to have with our visitors were either tedious or tense. There were also – a relief, under the circumstances – a few moments of farce. We were presented with a large number of well-meant but unwanted gifts, mostly boxes of chocolates, including two containing a brand called Good News.

Work provided a distraction, too. In principle I should have abstained from it; but I had recently begun writing a monthly feature about paperbacks for the *Times Literary Supplement*, and the next one was due. So every so often I slipped upstairs and banged away at my typewriter, and when the piece was ready I took it round to the *TLS* (which was still based in Printing House Square) by hand. In accordance with the laws of the shivah I had stopped shaving, and I showed up at the office with a four-day growth of beard. Today, it would probably be taken for designer stubble, and pass unremarked, but in 1960 I felt I had to explain why.

Some months later we assembled for the consecration of the tombstone. The inscription I had chosen, a verse from the Psalms, testified to my father's upright character. And after that it was over twenty years before I saw the cemetery again. When I did, many newer graves had naturally been added. One which caught my eye, was that of the East End boxer Kid Lewis: the inscription on the memorial stone said that he had 'taken the count' on such and such a day in 1971. My father's memorial stone was nearby. It had begun to weather.

15

Absolument moderne

As an adolescent I believed that one day I would find time to read everything. No doubt this was an extension of the fantasy most famously summed up by Hazlitt, when he wrote that 'no young man believes he shall ever die'; and, like that fantasy, it was not so much an active belief as an unstated assumption. Every so often, too, I would go to the other extreme, and feel overwhelmed by the thought of what a hopeless task it was to master even a tiny fraction of what a well-read person was supposed to have read. At such moments, which generally occurred in bookshops or libraries, it felt as though the books in front of me were about to fly up in my face, like the cards at the end of Alice's dream. Yet for a number of years, my original assumption persisted. There would always be time.

The assumption had two practical consequences. First, from early on I was drawn to literary history and books about books (or, more likely, essays about books). This may seem a paradox, since such things can often be a substitute for reading primary literature, a recognition that the alternative to second-hand knowledge of an author may well be no knowledge at all. But initially, at least, I approached them in much the same spirit that one might study a travel brochure or a guidebook – for an indication of pleasures to come. Second, the sense of limitless freedom encouraged my habit of promiscuous reading. Why worry about spending time on whatever book you fancied, when you were bound to read the classics sooner or later?

My principal motive in reading was curiosity. Taste wasn't

allowed to get in the way. Novels in particular – novels of almost any kind – promised to be so many keys to experience: I had already felt the power of Dostoevsky, but that didn't stop me becoming absorbed in a book called *Men Are So Ardent*, by Gerald Kersh. Much of what I read was determined simply by what caught my eye at the library, or what happened to be lying around. I read *Pip*, by Ian Hay, of which we had somehow acquired a Penguin, long before I read *Great Expectations*. And Penguins in general were indispensable. In those days the imprint seemed rather like the BBC: not so much a publisher as an estate of the realm. I was fascinated by the colour codes (navy blue for Autobiography and Memoirs, and so on); by the early Penguins you could still sometimes pick up (*Ariel*, *The Unpleasantness at the Bellona Club*), with advertisements in them; by the spin-offs, such as the Ptarmigan puzzle books; by the authors' notes on the back covers, with their revelations about who had worked as a lumberjack or a bartender, and who had won the John Llewelyn Rhys Prize or the Femina Vie Heureuse.

Nothing Penguins did gave me more pleasure, in the short run, than their big reissue of titles by Agatha Christie. (Green for Crime and Detection.) I had somehow missed out on mysteries since the days of Norman and Henry Bones, Boy Detectives, on the BBC. Now there was the thrill of discovering *The ABC Murders* – at the start of the summer holidays, too, so that long days stretched ahead, and I was soon following it up with *Lord Edgware Dies* and *The Mysterious Affair at Styles*, and marvelling at the ingenuity of *The Murder of Roger Ackroyd*. As it turned out, Agatha Christie was also to prove the first favourite author for whom I lost the taste: there wasn't enough atmosphere. By the time I had begun to cool, however, I had moved on to Ellery Queen, Ngaio Marsh and half a dozen others, and my fate as a mystery addict was sealed. And then came the golden day when I discovered Michael Innes, and realised that mysteries could be as sophisticated as I hoped ordinary novels would be. And beyond lay Raymond Chandler and the incomparable Simenon.

If I had kept a note of everything I read, the result would be fairly chaotic. But it would only tell part of the story. Some books obviously meant much more to me than others, and in terms of energy and attention my best efforts from the age of fifteen or so were devoted to the literature of what can most handily be described, though I dislike the term, as the modern movement.

I was lucky in being left free to discover the moderns pretty much for myself. I had been given an inkling of them at the Perse, mainly through the use of that Auden–Garrett anthology *The Poet's Tongue*. At the City of London, the English syllabus was old-fashioned. The big traditional names came first, and as far as I can recall the Eliots and Joyces were not even mentioned in passing – not until we were in the sixth form, at least. I was astonished when Kingsley Amis told me that in the thirties 'Boggy' Marsh, who was later my first form master at the school, had lent him copies of Auden and MacNeice. In my time Marsh was a decent but dry teacher. My chief memory of him in an English lesson is of him telling me that I shouldn't have begun a sentence in an essay with 'And', and, when I protested that I had come across H.G. Wells doing the same thing in a short story, coming back with the classic pedagogue's put-down that I should wait until I could write as well as Wells before I allowed myself to break the rules. But then he was also responsible for teaching us the first rudiments of Greek, and by the time I knew him he had probably been worn down by years of drilling small boys in the verbs in *-mi* and initiating them in the mysteries of the optative mood. (After he retired he took holy orders, ministered to a rural parish in the West Country and lived to a great age.)

Exploring the moderns under one's own steam was even more of an advantage than exploring *The Golden Treasury* had once been. One's relationship with them was so much more intimate and direct than it would have been if they had been set texts; so much more haphazard, too, and the more natural for being so. And the fact that they had not yet been admitted to the syllabus meant that they still had the aura of outsiders, challenging and subverting the literary status quo.

I must have belonged to the last generation for whom it was still possible to regard even T.S. Eliot in this light. It was largely an illusion: by the time I had begun to read him, he had won the Nobel Prize. But I was feeling my way, and when I came across examples of the resistance which he had initially aroused – Arthur

Waugh denouncing him as a drunken helot, for instance – I responded as though his opponents were still the force in the world they had once been, or something like it.

A number of paths drew me towards modernism, but the one I remember most clearly was a reading of Rimbaud's *Les Illuminations*, in the English translation by Helen Rootham (Edith Sitwell's friend and former governess: her versions are the ones which were set to music by Benjamin Britten). I had never heard of Rimbaud, and I am not sure what prompted me to take the book out of the library. Probably my eye was caught by the introduction, which was by Edith Sitwell, and which may have stirred memories of the 'Tango-Pasodoble' in *The Poet's Tongue*. At all events, when I began reading the poems I was immediately dazzled by the brilliant images, the strange juxtapositions, the dreamscapes and dream architecture (the marvellous façades of the Palais-Promontoire, 'the imperial brightness of the buildings'). They were dynamic, too, not just decorative: I could discern an impassioned voice in them, buried narratives, ordinary human emotions. I suppose the nearest thing to them which I had come across was *Kubla Khan*. But their imagery was more varied than Coleridge's, their procedures more dislocated. And the fact that they were in prose, yet unmistakably poems, seemed the crowning proof that any rule could be broken.

During my first wave of enthusiasm modernism essentially meant modern poetry. (James Joyce, still read only in extracts, counted as an honorary poet.) Modern painting was a separate but parallel discovery – Picasso and Paul Klee seemed to justify what I found in Eliot and Joyce, and vice versa – but it was the poets who beguiled me most. For a time, I assumed that anything which was commended or which advertised itself as modern had to be good, especially if it featured metrical and typographical irregularities. I remember puzzling over the poems of José Garcia Villa, whose gimmick was to insert a comma after every word. Before long, however, a more coherent picture began to emerge. I was guided primarily by anthologies, especially by the old Michael Roberts *Faber Book of Modern Verse* and the Kenneth Allott *Penguin Book of Contemporary Verse*, which had just come out. Then I began exploring individual writers. The peaks loomed up –

Mount Hopkins, Mount Late Yeats, Mount Early Pound. There were enticing foothills, and I was captivated by isolated poems, even though I didn't as yet know anything about the authors – Wallace Stevens' 'The Emperor of Ice Cream', for instance. But all roads led inexorably to Eliot.

I may not have had schoolmasters who drummed the importance of Eliot into me, but I didn't need them. No one in that era could read in or around modern poetry without quickly becoming aware of his unique standing. There was a poem for his sixtieth birthday written by Nicholas Moore which began:

> I read of Mr Eliot day and night.
> I read of him, I read, I read of him.

I know how Nicholas Moore felt. Eliot seemed to be everywhere. You weren't positively obliged to like him, but if you didn't, it would have been rather like being around in the early eighteenth century and not liking Pope.

My own pleasure in his work ran deep. There was no question of my liking it simply because I had been told to. And in spite of his celebrated doctrine of impersonality, many of the lines to which I responded most strongly were suffused with a romantic longing. 'Recalling things that other people have desired', for instance, or the childhood memories in 'Animula', 'running stags around a silver tray', or the end of 'Burnt Norton':

> Ridiculous the waste sad time
> Stretching before and after.

If I had been more confident, I would have acknowledged that I found *The Waste Land* and *Four Quartets* more problematic, less uniformly successful than 'The Love Song of J. Alfred Prufrock'. But the longer poems still lay at the heart of Eliot's achievement. They conferred authority on him: *The Waste Land* in particular was not just a *cri de coeur* but also, or so it seemed, a miniature epic of the modern world. And the sense of authority extended to his personality, and lent a glow of interest to everything about him. I was awed by the thought that he lived in the same city as I

did, that he took the Tube and worked in Russell Square. I
wondered whether I would ever have a chance to meet him.

Then there was Auden. As a man, as a figure, he didn't have the
mana of Eliot, the indefinable prestige which set him apart.
Perhaps he didn't want it. 'You were silly like us,' he wrote in his
poem on Yeats, and the phrase stuck in my mind. He was someone
who was willing, possibly even happy, to be thought fallible. He
was obviously extremely clever as well, a great juggler with ideas,
but clever in the way that a very clever schoolmaster was clever, or
Aldous Huxley: there was nothing mysterious about the lessons he
taught, nothing hard and implacable. Nor, I could see, did his
poetry have quite the weight of Eliot's, or Yeats's. But he was still
the modern poet who meant the most to me. In my mid-teens, I
was drunk on his work, and I haven't entirely sobered up even
now.

I began at the beginning. I picked up his *Poems*, 1930, in our
admirably well-stocked local library, skipped (for the moment) the
'charade' *Paid On Both Sides*, and started reading the first of the
shorter pieces:

Will you turn a deaf ear
To what they said on the sea shore ...

The impact was as great as that of the Rimbaud translations –
greater, because the rhythms were intrinsically English. That I
didn't understand the poem was a secondary consideration. It
plainly meant something. Exactly what could wait: meanwhile, it
was potent, and hypnotic, and the emotional significance of at
least some of its images and phrases seemed perfectly clear.

It would take twenty pages to explain the various ways in which
Auden appealed to me. My personal selection of his work would
find plenty of room for the conversational Auden, the rococo
Auden, the Horatian Auden, the balladeering Auden, the Kierke-
gaard-toting intellectual Auden. I am certainly not one of those
who think that his gift withered away when he went to America.
But in the end I would have to concede that his purest, most
concentrated work, or most of it, is to found in the poems he

wrote in the 1930s – among the kestrels and the gaitered gamekeepers, the ridges of rich apartments and the 'bankrupt countries where they mend the roads'; amid landscapes which were uniquely, unmistakably Audenesque, though as one read them they also seemed to rise up (such is the way with poetry) from deep within one's own experience.

To a schoolboy around 1950, the Auden of the thirties and the poets with whom he was associated belonged to that fabled era, just beyond the reach of memory, 'before the War'. This didn't make them feel in the least antique, however. Part of their attraction was not so much complicated modernism as simple modernity, in the sense that ordinary people understood it. They went along with everything which seemed most advanced or up to date about their decade – with streamlining, aviation, radio, electrification, documentaries, Bakelite, white-coated science, the white factories along the Great West Road, racing at Brooklands, 'new styles of architecture', the Shape of Things to Come. Impressed though I was by appeals to tradition, I was far from immune to the excitement of technological progress; and the fact that so many developments had been held up by the war meant that the modernity of the thirties still had much of its original futuristic gleam. Motoring, for example, remained a comparative novelty for me and references to it in the thirties poets struck a particularly powerful chord: Auden's 'smiling grimy boy in the garage', or MacNeice's

Regard these means as ends, concentrate on this Now,
And you may grow to music or drive beyond Hindhead
    anyhow . . .

Just like one of our own weekend excursions. I remember being annoyed by an old-guard critic who pounced disapprovingly on Cecil Day Lewis's line 'Down arterial roads riding in April'. He wanted to know, in the first instance, why it didn't scan, why the poet hadn't written 'Riding in April down arterial roads'. The answer seemed obvious. The broken rhythm was appropriate for riding on a motorbike, which is what Day Lewis was writing about: a conventional iambic pentameter would have been bland.

And although the line itself has a touch of thirties self-parody, at the time I found it fresh and bold. Indeed, there was still something rather exciting about arterial roads in themselves. (In 1950, if I had been vouchsafed a fast-forward glimpse of a motorway, I would have thought that it was one of the most glamorous things in the world.)

The landscape of the thirties poets was also the landscape of the Depression, of a pervasive unease, of impending war. This sense of crisis was an integral part of their power. They had responded to the challenge of fascism far more adequately than their poetic seniors, while in a loose fashion I accepted their critique of England as a sick society, or thought I did. But I didn't draw any hard political conclusions. Their frequently *communisant* opinions and activities in the thirties remained separate from what I felt about Communism in general. For one thing, they were poets, which earned them a degree of indulgence. For another, one could go along with the diagnosis (or part of it) without necessarily subscribing to the cure – and I wasn't sure quite how serious they were about the cure anyway.

There was a partial parallel in my attitude to Eliot. As an arraignment of the modern world, *The Waste Land*, for all that the Age of the Dictators had intervened, still had great force. As a political thinker, on the other hand, Eliot presented a much more mixed picture: he seemed to me partly a wise conservative, partly a reprehensible reactionary, partly neither here nor there. But then politics in the explicit sense, the politics that make people go out and vote, was not what one went to him for, and I found that his views, where I disagreed with them, could be comfortably disregarded.

With one exception – his references to Jews.

In discussing anti-Semitism, I have said little or nothing up to now of the place where I encountered it most frequently – on the printed page, and often in what Victorians would have called the Best Authors, too.

No one could read much English literature written before the second half of the twentieth century – or, as far as I can judge, much European and American literature, either – without coming across hostile characterisations of Jews, and derogatory remarks directed against them. Needless to say this isn't the whole story. Many authors of the past had nothing to say about Jews, one way or another. Many were sympathetic, often to the point of idealisation. Some were neutral. But neither was the hostility confined to the notorious cases, the authors who made it a deliberate part of their programme. On the contrary, it was more widespread than anyone could calculate. I had to brace myself for an ugly comment or insinuation dropping out of a clear blue sky.

Even in *Les Illuminations*, for example, there was a line lying in wait like a snake, in the very last poem in the book: '*A vendre ce que les Juifs n'ont pas vendu* . . .' 'For sale, what the Jews have not sold' (with the unmistakable implication that, given the chance, they would sell anything). Or, to take a darker instance, when I was eighteen I thought that *The Brothers Karamazov* was the greatest novel I had ever read. That it was a deeply Christian work, in no way made me feel cut off from it. I saw Alyosha Karamazov, the pure-hearted religious novice, as the equivalent of an ideal yeshiva *bocher*, a young Talmudic student. But I had read the book too quickly. I had overlooked the terrible passage in which the sick girl Lisa asks Alyosha whether it is true that Jews steal small children at Easter and kill them, and he replies, 'I don't know.'

And how did one respond to literary anti-Semitism? A number of resolutions, though I didn't consciously formulate them, took shape in my mind. Firstly, I would try to judge each case on its own merits. Secondly, I would neither ignore instances of prejudice, nor exaggerate them. Thirdly, I would be careful not to assume that they were necessarily the most important thing about the work in which they occurred. Fourthly, having noted them, I would reserve the right, in the lesser cases at least, to turn a blind eye: dwelling on them would simply ruin a lot of literature for me. Finally, I would always try to allow for the date at which something was written. That Chaucer, whom I loved, should have been so harshly anti-Jewish in 'The Prioress's Tale' was distressing, but it was a distressing fact about the fourteenth century rather than about Chaucer. On the other hand, any expression of anti-Semitism after Hitler was clearly worse than it would have been before.

A great deal has been written about Eliot in this connection in recent years. The contrast with the situation when I first got to know his work could hardly be greater. At that time, there was an eerie silence. You could read the classic early commentators, Edmund Wilson, F.O. Matthiessen and F.R. Leavis, to say nothing of dozens of lesser critics, without coming across any discussion of the topic at all.

The silence, as far as I was concerned, only aggravated the problem. And there *was* a problem, a painful one.

When I began reading Eliot, the anti-Semitic streak had been one of the first things that caught my attention. How could I have failed to notice the ferocities visited on the (lower-case) 'jew' in 'Gerontion', 'Sweeney Among the Nightingales' and 'Burbank with a Baedeker; Bleistein with a Cigar'? That such passages were unequivocally anti-Semitic, and nasty, I never doubted. But I was also content to think of them as no more than blemishes; and initially, if I am to be honest, I was as much intrigued as affronted. Here was something different – anti-Semitism with a smart new twist.

Or perhaps I was more shaken than I was willing to admit, since soon afterwards I felt impelled to mention the subject to my father. When I had had my say, either quoting or paraphrasing some offending lines, his only comment was, 'T.S. Eliot may be a great poet, but he isn't greater than the Jewish people.' I was very struck by this – not so much by the sentiment as by the manner in which it was expressed, which was very different from his normally low-key, non-rhetorical style. He was perfectly calm, but it was obvious he had been upset.

We let the subject drop. But I felt bad about it, and a couple of weeks later, as a tacit peace-offering, I read him Auden's philo-Semitic poem from the thirties, 'Refugee Blues'. His first reaction was rather tetchy. Why were German Jews the only ones Auden mentioned? What about other Jews? What about Jews from Eastern Europe? When I explained that the poem had been written before the war, however, he agreed that this was an unreasonable objection. Yes, Auden was clearly a good thing, and meanwhile I had established my general point that there was no necessary connection between modern poetry and obnoxious opinions.

The incident, or so it seemed, was closed. A few weeks went by. And then one day he suddenly remarked, with nothing in particular to prompt him, 'You know, T.S. Eliot would be very interested in a man like Abramsky.'

This was serious. Yehezkel Abramsky was the most renowned Talmudic scholar in London – probably the only one for whom my father felt the kind of unreserved respect he would have felt for the great masters back in Eastern Europe. Abramsky was the standard by which the others were judged.

My inward response was a mild sense of helplessness. I found the idea of Eliot's getting to know Abramsky so improbable that I wanted to smile. I found it hard to believe that he would have taken much interest in him if he had. That was not the way things worked. At the same time, the remark suggested that my father had been more disturbed than I had realised – and that he still was.

In terms of the culture in which he had grown up, Abramsky represented Authority; and I think he had intuited that for me Eliot represented Authority, too. In putting forward Abramsky's name, he was not necessarily trying to pit one Authority against another: he no doubt hoped that somehow, somewhere, the two could be reconciled. But the anti-Semitism which he might have regarded as a routine hazard in another writer was much more troubling in an author whom I gave the impression of looking up to as a lawgiver, a permanent point of reference.

Over the months and years which followed I naturally didn't forget about the anti-Semitic passages, but neither did I let them bother me unduly. Vivid and unignorable though they were, they amounted to no more than a few lines, and lines from fairly early poems (all written before 1921). There was so much else in Eliot's work, and so much, through his criticism, that he led on to.

At the same time my attitude towards the passages in question wasn't one of simple resignation. Every so often a feeling of anger would flare up, every so often I would look at them as though for the first time, and be aghast. I can even recall suddenly becoming annoyed with, of all things, *Old Possum's Book of Practical Cats*:

here was a work published on the eve of Hitler's war, in 1939, and it was all so ... cosy. On another occasion I was rereading 'Burbank with a Baedeker' –

> The rats are underneath the piles.
> The jew is underneath the lot.
> Money in furs ...

– when it occurred to me (I had never made the connection before) that my grandfather had been a furrier. What was I doing reading this miserable stuff?

If only there had been a retraction, some time after 1933 – or some time after 1934, the year in which Eliot published his notorious remark about 'free-thinking Jews' and how undesirable it was to have too many of them in a healthy society. What form such a gesture might have taken would of course have been for Eliot himself to decide. A few words, provided they had been deeply enough felt, would have done a great deal to defuse the situation. But no such words were forthcoming.

One of the appeals of modernism was that it was a means of maintaining the prestige of the arts in a changing world. It enabled one to believe that they were advancing on to new ground as decisively as science; that they reflected a new reading of human nature as revolutionary as Freud's. And modernism could also serve, up to a point, as a replacement for religion, or a substitute for a political creed.

I felt all these attractions myself, in varying degrees. There was a dizzying period when I thought there really had to be a clean break with the past: *il faut être absolument moderne*. That soon wore off. But the sense of taking part in a great forward movement remained – taking part as a reader, an appreciator and (who could say?) perhaps one day as a contributor, too.

Modern literature had also called forth a new race of critics. They were necessary: difficult writers demanded elucidation. At their best they were part of the modern movement themselves. The leaders of the profession were now stars, and lesser men felt buoyed up by their example. When Randall Jarrell, in an essay published around 1950, characterised the period as 'The Age of Criticism', everyone knew what he meant. Has there ever been a time when critics took so much pride in what they were doing, or felt so little need to defend themselves against the traditional charge that they were mere hangers-on, parasites? Jarrell was scathing about some of the consequences of this new climate – about the follies of criticism when it lost its sense of proportion, or when mediocre practitioners turned it into an industrial process. But he was a critic himself, one of the best of them.

Reading the primary writers, I was led on to the commentators. Reading the commentators, I found myself in a world both bracing and disconcerting, where analysis was being pushed to levels of subtlety I hadn't previously imagined, where a good deal that I had enjoyed or admired was rejected out of hand (my days of promiscuous reading were under threat), and where the map of the past was being drastically redrawn. I learned about little magazines and critical disputes; I caught my first whiff of Leavis.

Immersion in this new material could be very exciting. In some respects, indeed, it was not unlike discovering detective stories. (*Lehavdil*, as they say in Hebrew and Yiddish: 'if you'll forgive the comparison'.) Rightly or wrongly, I felt confident that modern-style criticism was a game I could play. And needless to say it was more than a game. It was being businesslike, where old-style critics had generally waffled. But I also held back. The romantic in me (or was it the realist?) still clung to the belief that the deepest effects of art were precisely those which defy analysis. You could celebrate a mystery, or compare it to other mysteries, or set it in context: the one thing you couldn't do was dissect it.

There was another kind of criticism, too, which in many ways I preferred – conversational, condensed, impressionistic, but not so passively impressionistic that it didn't make its critical and analytic points along the way; the kind of criticism that I found in the best literary journalism. I had taken to reading the *New Statesman* – in those days a notorious politico-literary pantomime horse – for the sake of its literary and artistic second half. At first I was bowled over; Friday (hooray!) was *New Statesman* day. Later, I decided that not all its reviews were as brilliant as I initially assumed. But I hadn't been wrong about V.S. Pritchett, who was then at the height of his powers as a critic, contributing essay-length reviews under the rubric 'Books in General'. They were as satisfying in themselves, artistically satisfying, as they were illuminating in their diagnoses. The first book of criticism I ever acquired, chosen by me for a school prize, was Eliot's *Selected Essays*. The second, paid for with my own money, was a second-hand copy of Pritchett's *The Living Novel*.

Pritchett and one or two of his journalistic colleagues made most academic criticism seem stiff-jointed and uninspired in comparison. But there were academic masters, too. *The Wheel of Fire* and *Seven Types of Ambiguity* were both great, if very different, discoveries. Empson in particular redeemed the notion of analysis. He was a poet primarily, or had been until his muse deserted him – an enormously gifted one. But for all his rich idiosyncrasy, he presented his readers with a critical method they could build on. He showed you how it should be done. And though he could be baffling – I often couldn't see how he had got from one sentence to the next – he was so entertaining that you forgave him. (One glimpse of him from a later period. When I took over at the *Times Literary Supplement* I was anxious to secure his services as a contributor, and he was one of the first people I called. 'Oh, it's you,' came his strange sing-song voice over the phone. 'Are you in the chair already?' 'Yes.' A long pause. '*Does it swivel?*')

Empson was quite unlike anyone else. But there he was, teaching and lecturing, soon to be a professor. The study of literature had largely migrated to the universities; and reading English had become a standard step for anyone dreaming of a literary career.

In principle my main subject, now I was in the sixth form, was history, but the school decided to put me in for a scholarship at Oxford in English – as a trial run, for the experience: the real test was supposed to come the following year. So in the spring of 1952 I went up to Wadham, a college of which I knew nothing (apart from the fact that it had a legendary Warden called Bowra), and spent two or three days writing papers, and drinking lots of coffee and looking around when I wasn't. In one paper, we were asked to compare two versions of a poem by Horace, without being told who the translators were, and I unerringly rejected the first version, which turned out to be by A.E. Housman, in favour of the second, which turned out to be by W.E. Gladstone. The rest of my stay in the college is largely a blur, apart from the interview, which took place late on the last afternoon.

The two men I sat facing, across a heavy desk, were my two future tutors – Humphry House, who seemed to have an almost Victorian weight and authority (strange to think that he was only in his early forties at the time), and John Bamborough, who was much younger, trim, ex-Royal Navy, lightly sardonic. There was a third figure sitting behind them who looked as though he might have been younger still, though it was hard to make him out in the shadows. We went through a few routine questions; then Humphry House asked me something about Empson, whom I had mentioned in one of my papers. I imagine he was trying to find out whether I had merely been dropping names, and although most of what I said in reply was probably muddled, it at least left him in no doubt that I had actually read *Seven Types of Ambiguity*, and that my enthusiasm was genuine. When I had finished, the mystery man in the shadows spoke for the first time: 'I can see what you say holds good for Donne or Pope, but do you think it really applies to someone like Tennyson?' – except that what he said was 'Te-te-tennyson', and I nearly jumped off the edge of my chair. It was John Bayley, then at the beginning of his Oxford career.

A few days later we heard that I had won the scholarship. I was naturally very pleased (although it took a while for it to sink in). My mother was delighted. My father was overjoyed. He drove over to tell his sister, and could barely restrain himself from phoning up everyone else in the family. 'This is *naches*,' he said, 'you've given us *naches*' (*naches* being an intensely Jewish word for satisfaction, especially the satisfaction which parents hope to get from their children).

There was still a term to go before I left school, but with exams no longer hanging over me, it passed quickly. I went for aimless walks, wandered over to Victoria Park, read Proust (or rather Scott Moncrieff), wondered about the future and what it held – about the fascinating friends I had yet to meet. At first I didn't think much about Oxford itself, but gradually I began to feel the lure of its mystique.

In September I went up to Wadham. Humphry House was to be my tutor for my first two terms, but John Bamborough was due to take over after that, and he asked me to come and see him in his rooms when I arrived.

It was a fine day, the sun was flooding in. 'Well,' he said after we had exchanged greetings, 'you did pretty well in your scholarship papers.'

'Thank you,' I said, trying to look as modest as possible.

'Buy yourself a bag of nuts,' he said – and my new life had begun.

John Gross is theatre critic of the (London) *Sunday Telegraph* and a former editor of the *Times Literary Supplement*. For a number of years he was also a staff writer for the *New York Times* in New York. His previous books include the classic study *The Rise and Fall of the Man of Letters* and the widely acclaimed *Shylock: Four Hundred Years in the Life of a Legend*. He has also edited several anthologies, among them *The Oxford Book of Essays* and *The Oxford Book of English Prose*. He lives in London.